HEAL
YOUR
GUT

HEAL YOUR GUT

LEE HOLMES

FAIR WINDS

FOREWORD

If our bodies were a royal court, the gut would be the quiet but powerful ruler sitting on the monarch's throne. I truly believe the gut is the seat of all health.

Lee Holmes knows firsthand how important the gut is to feeling your best, and in *Heal Your Gut* she shows the reader in a logical, stepwise fashion how healing your gut is the gateway to healing other health issues. Hippocrates said, "Let food be thy medicine," and what I love about Lee's approach is that when she reaches for her prescription pad, she is writing a recipe for healing through food, not pharmaceuticals. From my years of experience as a functional medicine practitioner in New York City, I have come to respect the power of food and the importance of a healthy and balanced gut ecosystem to overall health and wellbeing.

As the silent player in your health, your gut offers the greatest potential for healing – and also the highest potential for harm. Your gut is a fertile garden where both good and bad bugs can take root. With 100 trillion bacteria outnumbering our own cells ten to one, we are actually more bacteria than human. Involved at the root of a myriad of conditions – from chronic fatigue to autoimmune disease, fibromyalgia, migraines, prediabetes and weight gain – the gut and its resident microflora have been the most neglected organ system until now.

Within the wonderfully curated pages of *Heal Your Gut* you will find a plethora of practical advice; easy-to-understand steps; and recipes to detox, heal your body and feel great. Anyone who wants to improve their health should incorporate this approach to total body wellness. It all starts in your gut!

Vincent Pedre, M.D.
Author of *Happy Gut: The Cleansing Program to Help You Lose Weight, Gain Energy, and Eliminate Pain*

CONTENTS

MY HEALING STORY

Six years ago I was forced to make a radical life change after being diagnosed with a non-specific (that is, affecting several organs) autoimmune disease and fibromyalgia. In the first couple of years of my healing, the path was not easy. I spent three months lying in a hospital bed, coming to terms with the illness and the crippling arthritis. I lost more than 33 pounds (15 kg); hives and bruises covered my body from head to toe; and I suffered brain fog, hair loss and extreme fatigue. There were many days when I simply couldn't raise the energy to get out of bed.

Think of your gut as a garden that can only thrive when the soil is healthy. Healthy soil requires healthy foods and nutrients that will allow the "good guys" to flourish. By feeding my body all-natural, easily digestible wholefoods, I allowed it to heal at a fundamental level.

During my time in hospital I was given a concoction of drugs – everything from immunosuppressants and antibiotics to steroids, anti-cancer drugs and anti-inflammatories. This was all in an effort to get the inflammation in my body under control. The big problem was that the drugs made me feel worse, with their Alfred Hitchcock movie–like side effects! I was nauseated, tired, blurry and foggy. From my days studying nutrition, I always thought that many pharmaceutical drugs only mask the symptoms of disease. Most days when I woke up from an intermittent and interrupted sleep, I felt like a forty-year-old in an eighty-year-old woman's body – like Benjamin Button in reverse. I was bent double and unable to get out of bed, and my beautiful thick hair was falling out in clumps on my pillow.

As I lay there, I wondered if my condition could be diet-related and whether, if I healed my gut and gave my system a chance to recover, I would be able to regain my energy and health. I made a conscious decision to look more deeply at health and disease, to discover where my illness stemmed from and how I could heal myself naturally. Thus began the process of taking my medical destiny into my own hands. I was on a very restricted diet when I first got sick, because my body reacted to everything I ate and I'd started developing allergies and intolerances. So I began by eating lots of liquid foods, as I knew they would be easy to digest and my system would absorb their nutrients more effectively. This process of gently healing my gut lining took about four weeks, and it really gave my digestive system a chance to improve and recover.

After my gut felt better and I was in less pain, I started taking probiotics and eating probiotic-rich foods to heal my gut and replenish my gut microflora (my "good" bacteria). Once my gut began to heal, I started eating nutrient-rich foods. Soon I found I was ingesting more nutrients and absorbing them, and my health really took an upward turn. Think of your gut as a garden that can only thrive when the soil is healthy. Healthy soil requires healthy foods and nutrients that will allow the "good guys" to flourish.

I still have my autoimmune disease. Some days when it's raining outside or cold, my arthritic symptoms flare up, but I now know how to manage them, and they never interfere with my life like they used to. I live an energetic, healthy and full life, and the gut protocol I followed and the eating path I'm now on have changed my life for the better. I'm no longer on any prescription drugs and I'm 90 percent recovered. It would be untruthful to say that I'll ever feel 100 percent better, but a big part of my healing has been to accept my 90 percent, and in turn focus on enjoying every moment life has to offer.

Healing my gut was an integral part of regaining my health and vitality, and I want to share everything I've learned with you so that you too can heal your gut and get your life back.

1

THE VITAL IMPORTANCE OF YOUR GUT

"The road to health is paved
with good intestines."

SHERRY A. ROGERS, M.D.
HEALTH PROFESSIONAL AND AUTHOR

INSIDE YOUR GUT

To begin my expedition into healing the symptoms of my autoimmune disease naturally, I had to do a lot of research on the gut and how it affects your health. Your gut is not just your belly or your waistline, it's the gateway to the health of your brain and immune system. Two thousand years ago, Hippocrates – the ancient Greek physician – said, "All disease begins in the gut." It seems that now more than ever we should listen to this advice and look at the source of many of our health issues – the gut.

Hippocrates is known as the father of medicine, but modern-day medicine has drastically swayed from his concept, focusing on treatments rather than causes. While Hippocrates' message has been devastatingly overlooked for centuries, current research is beginning to point to the truth and depth of his simple idea. In fact, many researchers are beginning to say that supporting gut health and restoring the integrity of the gut barrier will be one of the most important goals of medicine in the twenty-first century.

GUT FLORA

Did you know that your body is host to around 100 trillion living organisms? Although you can't see them, you have a smorgasbord of bacteria *on* and *in* your body. They outnumber your own cells ten to one. They live in your hair, on your skin, inside your nose, your mouth – everywhere! But the largest concentrations of these teeny-tiny bacterial entities are in your gut.

The world within your gut involves a multifaceted, interconnected, interdependent relationship between living organisms called microflora. Microflora is the complex, diverse group of microorganism species that live in your digestive tract. These organisms, also referred to as gut flora, are most easily understood as fitting into the categories of either "good bacteria" or "bad bacteria."

"Good" or "friendly bacteria" perform a multitude of tasks within your body, but their common responsibilities include working to regulate the gut by neutralizing some of the toxic by-products of your digestion; preventing the growth of harmful, pathogenic bacteria; controlling your metabolism; reducing harmful substances such as carcinogens and toxins; gleaning and absorbing energy, nutrients and fatty acids from the foods you eat; recycling hormones; training the immune system; and communicating with your brain.

The world within your gut involves a multifaceted, interconnected, interdependent relationship between microorganism species . . .

"Bad bacteria" are microbes capable of causing disease in the body by producing infection and increasing cancer risk. Research has found that the presence of particular harmful bacteria in mice leads to overeating, metabolic damage and insulin resistance, highlighting a possible connection between bad bacteria and obesity and other weight disorders.

Researchers are finding out more and more about the important role of gut flora in overall health. Dysregulation of gut flora has been linked to the development of a range of illnesses, from autism and depression to autoimmune conditions such as Hashimoto's thyroiditis, inflammatory bowel disease (IBD) and type 1 diabetes.

A healthy balance of gut flora is approximately 85 percent good bacteria and 15 percent bad bacteria. However, our modern diet – which is high in sugar, carbohydrates, preservatives and additives – is the perfect breeding ground for overgrowth of bad bacteria that will kill off your healthy gut flora very quickly.

Other causes of this imbalance include modern medicines such as antibiotics, and drinking tap water, which contains chemicals including fluoride and chlorine that also kill off your good bacteria. If you suffer from acne, low energy, digestive problems or low immunity, chances are you have a gut-flora imbalance that needs to be rectified.

Current research by senior scientists at the American Gut Project in Colorado is investigating feces samples from a wide variety of people from around the world to match up their particular ecological community of gut microorganisms (called the microbiome or microbiota) with specific diseases. The hypothesis is that the human microbiome may be implicated in autoimmune diseases such as diabetes, rheumatoid arthritis, muscular dystrophy, multiple sclerosis and fibromyalgia.

CANDIDA AND THE GUT

An imbalance in your gut flora can lead to an overgrowth of a yeast called candida (*Candida albicans*), a type of fungus that lives naturally within the human body and aids digestion and nutrient absorption. When your candida levels are out of balance, the organism is kept in check by your good bacteria. If your microflora is imbalanced, however, candida can become destructive, breaking down the wall of the intestine and penetrating into the bloodstream, thereby releasing toxic by-products into your body that can cause a raft of debilitating symptoms. If you have an autoimmune problem there's a good chance you have an imbalance in your gut microflora and an overgrowth of yeast in your body.

Coconut oil is a heart-healthy saturated fat that balances cholesterol and supports immune system function. Coconut oil contains lauric acid, a proven antiviral, antibacterial and antifungal agent that's easily digested and absorbed. It helps the body eliminate toxins as well as improving digestion, and assists with the absorption of beneficial nutrients from our food. The best coconut oil to buy is one that's cold- or expeller-pressed and unrefined. It's the best oil to use for cooking as it has a high smoke point.

TEN COMMON CANDIDA SYMPTOMS

1 Chronic fatigue, lethargy, brain fog
2 Muscle and joint pain and fibromyalgia
3 Skin and nail fungal infections, athlete's foot or toenail fungus
4 Oral and vaginal thrush, urinary tract infections, rectal itching or vaginal itching
5 Irritable bowel syndrome (IBS) and digestive disturbances, such as bloating, gas, constipation or diarrhea, and new sensitivities to foods eaten regularly
6 Autoimmune diseases such as Hashimoto's thyroiditis, rheumatoid arthritis, ulcerative colitis, lupus, psoriasis, scleroderma and multiple sclerosis
7 Inability to concentrate, disorientation, poor memory, lack of focus, attention deficit disorder (ADD), attention deficit hyperactivity disorder (ADHD) and headaches
8 Skin and allergy problems such as sinusitis, itching, hay fever, eczema, psoriasis, hives, rashes and recurrent colds or tonsillitis
9 Heart palpitations, irritability, mood swings and anxiety or depression
10 Sugar and refined-carbohydrate cravings, sensitivities to chemicals and perfumes, alcohol intolerance and increased susceptibility to the side effects of medications.

SIMPLE YEAST TEST

Here's a simple test you can do to see whether yeast has overgrown in your body. It takes 15 minutes and all you need is a glass of water and a sample of your own saliva.

Here's how to do it:

1 Within 30 minutes of waking up, fill a glass with water and spit into it. Make sure you do it before you rinse, spit, or eat or drink anything.
2 Wait 15 minutes then determine your result:

* **NORMAL:** Your saliva floats on the surface.
* **HIGH LEVELS OF YEAST:** The glass is cloudy and your saliva sinks to the bottom like sediment. If your saliva floats but has tiny strings hanging down into the water that make it look like a jellyfish, or you see specks within the water, this could also mean you have too much yeast in your system.

If you're worried about your yeast levels, it's always best to visit your local integrative medical practitioner, who can take swabs, or blood, stool or urine samples to check for yeast overgrowth.

REBALANCING YOUR YEAST LEVELS

Candida and bad bacteria feed off sugar, so it's vitally important to avoid sugar for a period of time to kill off the bad bacteria in your gut. Any food that will break down into sugar very quickly – white bread, white rice – and a diet high in fruit or carbohydrates, such as pasta and even oats, will be a feast for bad bacteria. Avoiding these foods as much as possible for a period of time will starve bad bacteria and prevent them outnumbering friendly bacteria. If you're stumped as to how to create delicious sugar-free meals, you'll find lots of recipes in this book (look for the SF icon) and on my website – or check out my online bookshelf, which contains a bunch of sugar-free recipe books from wonderful sugar-free bloggers and authors.

Increasing your intake of dietary fiber, anti-inflammatory healthy fats – such as extra virgin olive oil, flaxseed (linseed) oil, cold-pressed extra virgin coconut oil and avocados – and increasing antioxidant-rich foods will help eliminate and destroy bad bacteria.

Garlic is a particularly potent natural antiseptic. It's been shown to be effective against 24 out of 26 strains of candida. It destroys unfriendly bacteria while boosting good bacteria. When I was healing my gut, garlic was one of my strongest allies.

Fiber-rich foods such as nuts and seeds, and an abundance of fresh vegetables including leafy greens, will sweep out candida and other yeasts from your system and have an alkalizing effect on the magical universe within, promoting a healthy gut-flora balance. Research from the University of Illinois has also shown that eating dietary fiber can have an impact on the health of our gut bacteria and promote a shift in our microbiome toward different types of beneficial bacteria. Fiber is fundamental for our gut ecosystem and helps it stay balanced.

For more drastic candida and other yeast elimination protocols, supplements such as oil of oregano, black walnut, burdock root, goldenseal, olive leaf extract, grapefruit seed extract and pau d'arco are terrific natural options. All are discussed in greater detail in the "Natural antibiotics and antimicrobials" section of this book (see page 75). Remember, it's really important to be aware that whenever taking supplements, you need to introduce them slowly and one at a time so that you don't overwhelm your body, and always follow your healthcare practitioner's advice with regard to dosages. The golden rule is not to jump into any anti-candida regimen too quickly.

Garlic is a particularly potent natural antiseptic. It's been shown to be effective against 24 out of 26 strains of candida. It destroys unfriendly bacteria while boosting good bacteria.

HEALING AND MAINTAINING A HEALTHY GUT BARRIER

It's good to know your internal flora status, and there are tests available for you to find out exactly what levels of certain bacteria are residing in your gut. Gut *flora* is, however, only one side of the gut-health story. Healing and maintaining a healthy gut *barrier* is another highly important factor.

The gut barrier reaches from your mouth all the way through to your anus, and its primary focus, aside from transporting and eliminating food and water, is to prevent foreign, unwanted substances from entering the body. The gut barrier must therefore remain strong and healthy in order to perform this function. Unfortunately, due to unhealthy modern lifestyles, gut permeability or "leaky gut" is becoming a common problem. This involves the breaking down of the intestinal walls, creating "holes" that allow large protein molecules to escape into the body. Because these substances are not supposed to live outside the walls of the gut, the immune system views them as invaders, mounting an immune response that aims to attack these proteins. This phenomenon is believed to be a primary culprit in the rise of autoimmune conditions. I noticed that as soon as I started healing my gut lining, my symptoms began to disappear.

Although conventional medicine in the past scoffed at this idea, many medical experts and researchers are now beginning to recognize that the integrity of the intestinal barrier is paramount in preventing and healing a range of diseases.

A really important point for you to remember on your own healing pathway is that the way to heal the gut involves a dual focus: improving the balance of good bacteria in the gut, *and* healing the intestinal walls to decrease intestinal permeability. By doing this you're allowing your gut to smoothly complete all of the functions required to regulate your entire body, without leaking unwanted toxic substances into the bloodstream, and thus minimizing your risk of developing various diseases.

THE GUT AND IMMUNE SYSTEM CONNECTION

All the systems within your body work closely together to maintain optimal health, so when one system is unbalanced it can trigger a domino effect, causing problems in other areas of your body and creating a cascade of chronic health complications. This is particularly true of the gut and its impact on immune health. Your gut health and immune system are inextricably linked. Did you know that 70–80 percent of your immune tissue is located within your digestive system? The gut is often the first entry point for pathogens (bad bacteria and viruses that can cause disease); your gut immune system therefore needs to be thriving and healthy in order for you to avoid illness. This was one of the key drivers to my own healing – knowing that if I could heal my gut, my symptoms would start to improve.

Your immune system is your first line of defence. Without a healthy balance of good bacteria in the gut, your immune system can't do its job effectively, and in essence is defenceless.

The digestive system is comprised of cells, proteins, tissues and organs that work together in a complex way to defend the body against harmful bacteria, infectious diseases and toxins. In fact, the gut mucosa that forms the intestinal barrier connects with the largest population of immune cells in the body, known as gastrointestinal immune cells. These come from the lymphoid branch of the immune system and they include lymphocyte cells that attack harmful invaders. These lymphatic cells also form bundles known as Peyer's patches, which work together to protect the mucous membranes of the small intestine from infection. They do this by releasing specific white blood cells (lymphocytes) known as T-cells and B-cells to defend the inside of the digestive tract from infection, as well as repair the damage that bad bacteria cause to the intestinal walls.

The intestinal barrier is also home to friendly gut flora that are critical for overall immunity. These guys act as mighty warriors for the immune system, and are dependable allies for immune cells, helping them enhance their "natural killer" effectiveness and boosting their overall defence of the intestinal walls so as to prevent pathogens and infections

HOW TO MAKE SLIPPERY ELM PORRIDGE

Place 1–2 tablespoons slippery elm inner bark powder in a blender with $\frac{1}{4}$ teaspoon powdered stevia, $\frac{1}{2}$ teaspoon vanilla essence, $\frac{1}{4}$ teaspoon cinnamon and 1 cup (9 fl oz/ 250 ml) of almond milk and blend until smooth. Pour the mixture into a small saucepan, and over low heat bring it gently to a simmer, stirring constantly until it thickens to the consistency of soft porridge. Remove from the heat, spoon into a bowl and eat immediately.

Slippery elm has been used as both food and medicine in many herbal traditions, including Native American, Ayurvedic, traditional Chinese and Western medicine. It's extremely nourishing to the body and can be eaten as a meal.

from entering the bloodstream. This is why maintaining a healthy balance of good bacteria in the gut is so important. Without them, your immune system can't do its job effectively, and in essence is defenceless.

HEALING A LEAKY GUT

A variety of illnesses can occur when these protective functions of the gut are compromised. As discussed earlier, intestinal permeability or 'leaky gut' causes the immune system to go into overdrive, mounting an unnecessary response against things like gluten, bad bacteria and undigested foods that have passed through these permeable holes in the gut lining. One of the first indications of leaky gut is the rise of food intolerances. If left unhealed, this can lead to immune abnormalities and eventually autoimmune conditions and other health issues. Some of these include IBD, arthritis, eczema, psoriasis, depression, migraine headaches, muscle pain and fibromyalgia, chronic fatigue, colitis, type 1 diabetes, Graves' disease, thyroiditis, multiple sclerosis, lupus, scleroderma, Crohn's disease and Addison's disease.

If you think you may have leaky gut, nourishing slippery elm porridge (see opposite) will really help you to seal your gut lining. The herb slippery elm has been shown to neutralise acidity, and acts as a soothing demulcent by coating the membrane surface and protecting mucous membranes along the gastrointestinal tract. Slippery elm porridge really helps to soothe irritated intestines by isolating the acidic environment, and promoting tissue regeneration. It helps with constipation and doesn't cause bloating. Slippery elm has been used as both food and medicine in many herbal traditions, including Native American, Ayurvedic, traditional Chinese and Western medicine. This porridge is extremely nourishing and can be eaten as a meal. If your leaky gut is particularly troublesome, eat it three times a day for three days to really help promote gut healing and then return to eating it as a meal replacement when needed. You can also make a small drink with 1 teaspoon slippery elm powder and ½ cup (4 fl oz/ 125 ml) warm water to be taken half an hour before meals.

It's only in recent years that scientists have begun to discover the vital importance of the links between diet, gut bacteria and the immune system. Scientific evidence now shows that the types of food you eat directly determine the levels of certain bacteria in your gut. Changing your diet will change the kind of bacteria you have, which will either support the strengthening of your immune system or deplete its defensive capabilities. Conclusions drawn from the current research all reveal that a healthy immune system is the result of a diet that supports healthy gut function – one that emphasises whole, unprocessed foods and helps repopulate the gut with good bacteria.

THE GUT AND BRAIN CONNECTION

The gut is not only deeply connected to your immune system; the health of your digestive system will directly impact the functioning of your brain. This is known as the gut–brain axis, and highlights the interdependency between these two areas of the body. In fact, your body has *two* nervous systems: the central nervous system, which is composed of your brain and spinal cord; and the enteric nervous system, which is the intrinsic nervous system of your gastrointestinal tract.

Your two nervous systems are formed at the same time during fetal development, and are created from identical tissues, connected via the vagus nerve. This is the tenth cranial nerve, which runs from the brain stem right down to your abdomen, and is the primary route your gut bacteria use to transmit messages to your brain. Knowledge of the vagus nerve completely flips the idea that the brain controls the rest of your body. Rather, it reveals that your gut is largely in charge. In fact, your gut sends far more information to your brain than your brain sends to your gut!

Just as you have neurons in your brain, you also have neurons within your gut. This includes neurons that produce neurotransmitters such as serotonin. Serotonin is the neurotransmitter responsible for feelings of wellbeing and happiness, and it's found in its greatest concentration within the gut, not the brain itself. When my autoimmune disease first flared up I had terrible symptoms of anxiety and depression. This was partly due to the steroids I was taking and to the anxiety of being sick, but also because my gut didn't have the correct balance of microflora and wasn't functioning properly.

The ability of the gut microbiota (the community of microorganisms in your gut) to communicate with the brain and influence behaviour is emerging as a very exciting concept in the scientific world of health and disease. Research proves that your own unique combination of microflora interacts with *you* as the host to form essential relationships that govern the balance and functioning of your entire body. There's no doubt that the presence of good bacteria in the gut alters brain function. Research has gone so far as to show that the presence of a particular strain of bacterium known as *Bifidobacterium longum* NCC3001 removes anxiety-like behavior in mice. Other fascinating scientific findings include the ability of certain probiotics to modulate antidepressant-like behavior by reducing pro-inflammatory cytokines (cell-signalling proteins) and increasing levels of tryptophan (an amino acid, one of the building blocks of protein), both of which have been implicated in depression.

The close connection between stress-related psychiatric symptoms such as anxiety and gastrointestinal disorders like IBD provide further proof that the gut–brain axis exists. The impact of poor gut health on the functioning of the brain has been scientifically linked to a range of illnesses including ADHD, autism, chronic fatigue, obsessive compulsive disorder (OCD), Tourette syndrome, and anxiety and depression. Good gut health is without a doubt paramount in the state of your mind; once I started paying attention to my gut, my anxiety and depression dissipated.

Research continues to link the state of the gut to many modern-day illnesses. It seems that Hippocrates was right all along. And the key to maintaining the health of the gut can be found in another of Hippocrates' wise statements: "Let food be thy medicine, and medicine be thy food."

You know the truth by the way it feels. Listen to your gut.

FACTORS THAT DAMAGE THE GUT

The vast number of gut-related health conditions that have arisen in the last century reveals the negative impact our post-industrialized diet and lifestyle are having. Science now shows that a number of nutritional health effects are mediated by intestinal bacteria, and that diet and lifestyle are key in influencing the composition and activity of these bacteria. Likewise, the breakdown of the intestinal walls that leads to leaky gut has been linked to specific nutritional factors that are a major component of our modern Western lifestyle.

GLUTEN

One of the most highly consumed foods in the Western world is gluten-containing grains, particularly wheat. Due to agricultural politics, wheat and other gluten-containing foods are one of the highest priorities on the food pyramid. Mainstream media will always hail whole grains as some of the healthiest foods you can consume for true health. When it comes to the health of your gut, however, especially if it's compromised, consuming wheat, or any other food containing gluten, can cause serious damage to your intestinal walls.

Research conducted by the Mucosal Biology Research Center at the University of Maryland in 2006 concluded that gliadin (a protein in the gluten fraction of wheat) can cause intestinal permeability in both celiac and non-celiac mucous membranes. This study proved that wheat gluten activates signalling by zonulin (a protein responsible for modulating the structure and permeability of the gut lining) in a way that creates permeable holes within the gut wall. The most interesting part of this study revealed that regardless of whether your autoimmune condition is the result of gene expression or of other factors, gliadin contributes to intestinal permeability in all people. In other words, if you're trying to improve the health of your gut, you'll need to avoid wheat and all other forms of gluten.

The hybridization and recent mass consumption of the wheat grain is believed to be one of the main reasons these gluten-induced gut problems are arising. The wheat we consume today has quite a different composition from the wheat consumed forty years ago. In the 1970s the old bread wheat grain was subjected to intensive rounds of hybridization experiments in order to solve some of the world's hunger problems. The new genetically altered wheat grain contains far more gluten than the original grain and produces ten times the yield of the old Einkorn grain grown in the fertile crescent of the Middle East.

Sadly, this new form of wheat has made its way into Western agriculture and is the most prevalent form of wheat we have today. It provides manufacturers with the greatest yield at the lowest price. Unlike the old Einkorn grain it doesn't grow in the wild. It's the result of domestication, intervention and fertilization by humans. This modern-day wheat has been internally and structurally changed. Our bodies aren't used to this change and, given wheat's mass consumption, this explains the dramatic spike in autoimmune conditions in the last few decades.

Because wheat dominates the diet of so many people, gluten in all forms should be restricted in order to heal and repair your gut. Gluten can't be easily digested, which means it gradually deteriorates the gut lining, causing leaky gut. When gluten leaks through the gut it can disrupt organ function, causing problems including fatigue, a foggy brain, and feelings of anxiety and depression, which is exactly what happened in my case.

FOODS AND OTHER PRODUCTS THAT CONTAIN GLUTEN AND WHEAT

These include:

* baked goods (almost all forms)
* packaged foods and breakfast cereals
* beer
* salami and cured meats
* muesli and muesli bars
* vinegar and soy sauce
* instant meals, frozen foods
* most breads
* baby food
* salad dressings
* sausages
* packaged chips and crackers
* lipstick and cosmetic products

Several additives and sweeteners, such as glucose syrup, are gluten- and wheat-derived. It's best to avoid all additives if you aim to heal and restore your gut. Stick to gluten-free wholefoods that are free from artificial preservatives and additives. I noticed that as soon as I omitted gluten from my diet, my digestive system felt a lot more at ease and my symptoms were less severe.

Further down the track, when your gut is healed, you can reintroduce gluten into your diet if that works for you.

ANTIBIOTICS

Before I was diagnosed with an autoimmune problem I had recurrent episodes of cystitis. Each time I had an attack I would go to the doctor and he would offer me a script for broad-spectrum antibiotics, which I would take diligently. This, I believe, was why I developed an autoimmune disease. While antibiotics can be vital in treating life-threatening conditions, they're not without their side effects. The role of the antibiotic is to kill off bad bacteria, but it also takes the good with the bad. The over-prescription and overuse of antibiotics is believed to be causing serious long-term consequences to our health due to its negative impact on the levels and diversity of our precious microflora.

The decrease in good bacteria can be responsible for the overgrowth of bad bacteria and pathogens relating to illness. Antibiotics are known to cause diarrhea, which may be due to infection by antibiotic-resistant pathogens such as salmonella, staphylococcus and possibly candida, as well as to the various consequences of reducing concentrations of friendly gut flora. If you have an illness such as cystitis or the flu (which is caused by a virus, against which antibiotics have no effect) that can be treated without the use of broad-spectrum antibiotics, I recommend that you explore natural options for recovery where possible. Where antibiotics are necessary, a qualified integrative doctor or naturopath should be able to supply you with probiotic support and detoxifying herbs such as milk thistle to help recolonize your intestines with some of the lost beneficial bacteria. Other prescription medications that disrupt the balance of your microflora are steroids (including corticosteroids such as prednisone and hydrocortisone), non-steroidal anti-inflammatory drugs (NSAIDS), antidepressants, laxatives and antacids.

INFECTION

Infections from unfriendly microbes and bad bacteria cause an overgrowth of bad microbes to outnumber the good guys. When harmful bacteria thrive in the case of an infection, you may experience persistent urinary tract infections, and thrush and yeast infections. When pathogens thrive and outnumber the friendly gut flora, this has an effect on overall immunity, which can cause a cascade of other problems and further infections. The aim is to create an environment where your beneficial microflora eventually numbers in the trillions of individual cells, creating a harmonious, complex relationship that drives a healthy immune system, a healthy brain and overall vitality.

STRESS

Stress can be very detrimental to the health of your gut. Have you ever had stomach discomfort before giving a speech? This is proof of the connection between the stress response and the digestive system. This kind of short-term stress can be dealt with, but consistent stress responses over the long term will cause a range of negative effects, including a decrease in nutrient absorption, decreased oxygenation of the gut, four times less blood flow to your digestive organs (it moves to the limbs, so they can "run away" from a potential threat), decreased metabolism and negative effects on microflora. Some really wonderful ways I've learned to de-stress are introducing yoga and meditation into my life, and having a morning routine. Meditation and deep breathing help calm the gut and balance your gut–brain connection.

EXTERNAL TOXINS

Irritants and toxic substances that can upset the balance of gut flora and damage the gut lining come in many forms, such as processed foods and foods containing chemicals, preservatives, flavors and additives. Artificial sweeteners are one ingredient to really avoid, along with nitrites and carcinogenic foods. Skin, hair, body and home-care products also contain high levels of toxic ingredients that can cause internal damage. You can find out more about this in the "Detox your life" section (see page 90).

KISS FOOD ADDITIVES GOODBYE

Food additives are chemicals added to the food we eat to keep food as fresh as possible, prolong its shelf life, and enhance its color, texture or flavor. Since the advent of processed foods, many more artificial additives have been introduced into our food. In Europe additives are assigned an "E" number for regulation purposes. Outside Europe the "E" before the number is sometimes dropped and just the number is used. It's tricky when navigating food labels to truly understand what's in our food, especially when the wool is pulled over our eyes. What's even trickier is that some of the additives in our food are naturally derived, like yellow coloring from turmeric.

If you have a sensitive gut, you're more likely to react to artificially created additives. Such reactions can include an array of symptoms, from hives, skin rashes and breakouts to digestive disorders such as diarrhea, stomach pain and bloating, and respiratory problems such as asthma and wheezing.

Food additives come in all shapes and sizes but can be categorized depending upon the job they do within our food. Some of the main food additives are:

* **FOOD ACIDS:** commonly added to food to enhance its taste and flavor. They also act as preservatives and antioxidants. Common food acids include vinegar (acetic acid), citric acid, tartaric acid, malic acid, fumaric acid and lactic acid. One to watch out for is artificially produced citric acid, also known as E330 or 330. Artificial citric acid can contain genetically modified organisms, mold and sulfites, to which people may have allergies. It's often added to cakes and biscuits; canned soups and sauces; frozen, packed and canned food products; and confectionery and ice cream.

* **ACIDITY REGULATORS:** used to alter the acidity and alkalinity of foods. They also act as emulsifiers.

* **ANTICAKING AGENTS:** added to help stop powders caking or sticking together to form clumps.

* **ANTIFOAMING AGENTS:** added to help reduce or prevent foaming in foods.

* **ANTIOXIDANTS:** such as vitamin C, used as a preservative by inhibiting the effects of oxygen in food. Some antioxidants to step away from are gallates 310–312, tert-butylhydroquinone (TBHQ), butylated hydroxyanisole (BHA) and butylated hydroxytoluene (BHT) 319–321. BHA and BHT are two

preservatives used for color retention and to prolong shelf life. These neurologically disturbing additives can be found in vegetable oils, cereals, potato chips, confectionery and chewing gum.

* **ARTIFICIAL COLORS:** used to replace colors that can be lost during processing, or to create visual appeal. Common foods containing artificial colors and food dyes are children's foods and processed foods such as soft drinks, fruit juices, salad dressings, hot dogs, cereals, confectionery and baked goods. Steer well clear of 102, 107, 110, 122–129, 132, 133, 142, 143, 151, 155 and 160b (annatto) if you want to avoid unnecessary reactions.

* **BULKING AGENTS:** such as starch, added to contribute to the bulking of a food without affecting its nutritional value.

* **EMULSIFIERS:** used to help water and oils form an emulsion and not separate. They are found in many foods, including mayonnaise, ice cream and homogenized milk.

* **FLAVOR ENHANCERS:** used to enhance a food's taste. They may be extracted from natural sources through distillation, solvent extraction or maceration, or created artificially. Some flavor enhancers detrimental to health include glutamates and monosodium glutamate (MSG) 620–625, disodium guanylate 627, disodium inosinate 631, ribonucleotides 635 and hydrolyzed vegetable protein (HVP). Yeast extract, hydrolyzed vegetable protein (HVP) and hydrolyzed plant protein (HPP) are all ways manufacturers use to include MSG without having to declare it on the label. Cheeky!

* **PRESERVATIVES:** very common food additives that are mostly used to prevent or inhibit spoilage of food due to fungi and bacteria. When you've got your magnifying glass out, check on food labels for sorbates 200–203, benzoates 210–213, sulfites 220–228, nitrates, nitrites 249–252, propionates 280–283, and whey powder in bread.

* **STABILIZERS, THICKENERS AND GELLING AGENTS:** such as agar or pectin, used to bulk food up, give it a firmer texture and increase its viscosity. Carrageenan 407, guar gum 412, methylcellulose 461, 464, 465, 466 and xanthan gum 415 are best avoided, especially if you have an ailing digestive system.

On your next trip to the supermarket check the labels on your food to ensure you're leaving these unnatural foods on the shelf. If we all refuse to buy them we can reduce demand for these items and increase demand for wholesome, fresh and unadulterated food.

2

HEALING AND TREATMENT PROTOCOL

Follow your own inner compass.
It will guide you.

THE FOUR PHASES OF GUT HEALING

Now that you understand your gut's connections to the other systems within your body, it's a good time to get practical with how you can heal your own gut and bring about optimal health. There are four phases to healing the gut and improving your health, so let's get straight to it.

1 HEAL YOUR INTESTINAL WALLS

Give your digestive system a rest by reducing all heavy and hard-to-digest foods that will irritate your gut. Follow a four-week anti-inflammatory elemental diet to supply your body with key nutrients, using smoothies, juices, soups, stocks, mashes and nutritional supplements. Think of your gut as a garden where you are planting seeds, then watering and tilling the soil.

2 DETOX YOUR BODY

Aid the detoxification of your body by oil pulling, Epsom salts baths, dry skin brushing and gentle movement. Very gradually include a natural antimicrobial to kill off yeasts and bacteria. Cleanse and sweep out your gut, support your liver while detoxing and reintroduce solid foods at your own pace. Pull out your garden's noxious weeds to make way for healthy new life to be planted.

> "There is more wisdom in your body than your deepest philosophies."
>
> FRIEDRICH NIETZSCHE

3 START A LONG-TERM HEALTHY DIET

Repopulate your gut with healthy microflora and eat foods that promote healthy bacteria. Digestive enzymes can be used to help your body break down food and minimize your symptoms. Fertilise your inner garden with naturally abundant probiotic-rich foods.

4 DETOX YOUR LIFE

Resolve any outstanding emotional issues, learn self-care and to love and nurture yourself, and develop an attitude of gratitude for everything you have. Plant perennials, annuals and evergreens, and allow your inner garden and spirit to flourish.

Let's break down each phase and look at it in more detail. The first and most important stage in achieving a healthy gut is to heal your intestinal walls and create an environment where bad bacteria, candida and other yeasts cannot survive or dominate. The following plan will rectify any permeable holes that may be leaking undigested food into your bloodstream, and create a strong "net" that will provide a safe home for your microflora.

The gut wall acts as the gatekeeper to decide what stays in and what stays out, so it needs to be healed and healthy. Fortunately, the surface microvilli in the small intestine (little lumps all over the inner surface that vastly increase its absorption capacity) are highly regenerative. If given total rest from everything that irritates and inflames them, they can recover fully in a matter of weeks. I noticed a dramatic increase in my overall health once the health of my gut was restored. It's really important to make changes in your own time and listen to your body and what it's trying to tell you. Try not to force anything if it doesn't feel right.

This book is just a guide for you to create your own healing plan. Don't beat yourself up if you fall off the wagon; it's completely natural to do that from time to time and to give in to cravings. Just take each day as it comes, allow your body the time and space to heal, and don't be too hard on yourself. If you prefer to undertake the four-week protocol with others, join the Heal Your Gut program on my website. You'll make friends and enjoy additional support.

PHASE ONE

THE ELEMENTAL DIET

GUT-HEALING PROTOCOL

To heal your gut to a healthy state, you'll need to undertake an elemental (liquid) diet for four weeks. This is what I did to heal my gut and it was the absolute key to my healing. When I talk about a liquid diet I don't mean a juice cleanse or a fad diet, I mean nutritious, easily digestible meals that your body will be able to absorb. This four-week protocol involves consuming liquid meals that still taste great but don't lack nutrients or satiety, and are easier on the digestive system. There was a lot of trial and error involved at the time, but after much research, experimentation and speaking with integrative doctors and nutritionists, I came up with the optimum way to heal and transform my gut naturally so that my body could in turn heal and my immune system could strengthen itself. After giving my body a four-week break from digesting solid food, it was amazing how my gut lining healed and became less inflamed. This in turn enabled me to absorb more nutrients, which gave me an increase in energy and a decrease in symptoms.

FOODS TO AVOID

The first and most obvious thing I did was avoid all the foods and lifestyle factors that damage the gut and promote the growth of harmful bacteria and yeasts. These are described in more detail in "Factors that damage the gut" in Part One.

I also avoided foods that feed bad bacteria and yeasts during this period, as well as foods that continued to inflame my gut. These foods may be different for each individual, so it's important to go on an elimination diet if a particular food is bothering you, even if it's a healthy food, and see if your symptoms improve. Keep a food diary to manage and revisit your observations. The aim is to give your digestive tract a well-needed rest from hard-to-digest foods and foods that cause inflammation and irritation.

For me, those foods included:

* any sweetener, sugar or fruit that contains fructose. This includes honey, agave syrup, maple syrup, refined and unrefined sugar and all fruits except lemons and limes. If you need to satisfy a craving for fruit, the best ones to consume are berries, which cause the smallest number of problems. If they're a problem for you and you see an increase in symptoms, it's better to avoid them altogether for four

weeks and reintroduce them after your gut has healed and your symptoms have reduced.

* starchy vegetables, including beets, carrots, parsnips, potatoes, squash, sweet potatoes and yams. Cut these out for the first four weeks, then reintroduce them at your own pace.
* dairy and milk products in all forms, including goat's and sheep's milk products. Butter can be included if it doesn't cause symptoms. You can reintroduce goat's and sheep's milk products after the initial four-week period, depending upon how you feel.
* nuts and seeds, but nut milks are okay if they don't give you any symptoms. You can warm up nut milk to create beautiful healing and nourishing warm drinks. Try the Anti-inflammatory Toddy on page 128.
* all grains, including rice, corn, millet, buckwheat, quinoa, wheat, couscous, amaranth, kamut, spelt, rye and barley. Once your gut is healed and depending upon your own preference, you can reintroduce grains that have been prepared through such methods as soaking, sprouting and fermenting. By using these preparation methods you're helping the process of breaking down the anti-nutrients (substances that prevent you absorbing nutrients) such as phytic acid, so that the grains become more digestible.
* hard-to-digest beans and lentils, which only put strain on your digestive system at this point. They can be eaten at a later time if sprouted and soaked, preferably overnight or for at least eight hours.
* caffeinated drinks, including coffee and chocolate-based drinks. Remove the buzz and alleviate the demands it places on your overtaxed adrenal glands. Caffeine also fools your fatigue factor, and diminishes healing and detoxification efforts.
* bad fats. The most damaging fats and oils for the body are man-made hydrogenated fats (e.g. trans fats) and polyunsaturated fats and vegetable oils. The hydrogenation process results in an extremely toxic product that the body finds difficult to process. Steer clear of vegetable fats and oils, such as canola (from rape seed), soy, safflower, sunflower, soybean and corn oils. Many products contain these fats and oils, such as margarine, salad dressings, mayonnaise, and cooking and baking oils. It's good to get used to reading food labels too, as oils can be blended together.

If your gut problems stem from candida overgrowth, it's best to avoid

SUPERCHARGED TIP

If you're following a low-FODMAP diet for food intolerances and have a problem with eating garlic and onion because they make you bloated or cause discomfort, you can replace garlic and onion in the recipes with the green part of a scallion, chives or the Indian herb asafoetida. Remember to chop it fairly finely and see how your body reacts.

fermented foods and foods derived from fungus, such as soy sauce, tempeh, miso, cheese, mushrooms, alcohol, vinegar and fermented vegetables. You can reintroduce fermented foods after the four-week protocol or when your gut is ready, but you should do this only in small quantities and when you can tolerate them. There are some fun fermented recipes in the book for you to try when you get to that stage (see page 229).

When your symptoms have abated and your gut flora is once again in balance, you can reintroduce some of these foods into your diet following the 80/20 rule, which is to eat well 80 percent of the time and allow yourself 20 percent wiggle room.

FOODS TO INCLUDE

To give your digestive system time to recover and heal itself, you'll need to consume all the following foods in liquid form for four weeks, whether they're fed through a juicer, processed in a blender, mashed or squished. Think freshly squeezed vegetable juices, soothing soups, nutrient-packed smoothies, healing broths and slurpable sorbets. You'll find lots of healing recipes in Part Three. If you're confused or suffering from brain fog, there are weekly meal planners on pages 52–63 for you to follow; they will inspire you with ideas over the four-week healing period.

Good foods include:

* non-starchy vegetables such as artichokes, asparagus, broccoli, brussels sprouts, cabbage, green beans, fennel, cauliflower, turnips, radishes, celery, cucumber, eggplant, onions, avocados, zucchini and button (pattypan) squash. Load up on these and make them into warming, delicious, healing soups.

SUPERCHARGED TIP

The best olive oil to use is cold-pressed extra virgin olive oil, which, as it originates from the first pressing of the olives, is high in quality and contains more nutrients. Look for dark bottles, which protect the oil from damage by light. Because olive oil is damaged by heat, it's best used unheated in salad dressings and homemade mayonnaise, or poured over foods after they're cooked. You can make your soups with it, if you cook them over a moderate temperature. Adding butter raises the smoke point of olive oil, allowing you to cook at hotter temperatures. Coconut oil can be used at higher temperatures.

EAT FOODS THAT TICK THE RIGHT BOXES

EAT LESS CRAP

Carbonated drinks
Refined and processed sugars
Additives, artificial colors, flavors
and sweeteners
Processed and packaged foods

EAT MORE REAL FOOD

Fermented food, low-fructose fruits
and vegetables
Organic and unprocessed foods
Omega-3 fatty acids
Drinks such as herbal teas and
filtered water

* leafy green vegetables. They will be your best friend during these four weeks. They're low in sugar, highly detoxifying, nutrient-dense and energy-boosting, so pack dark leafy greens such as arugula, spinach and kale into your juices and smoothies. A bit of lemon or lime will take off any bitter edge.
* avocados, lemons and limes and the occasional serving of berries. These should be the only fruits you eat for the first four weeks.
* anti-inflammatory, detoxifying and immune-boosting herbs and spices, such as basil, parsley, cilantro, black pepper, turmeric, cinnamon, cloves, dill, mint, garlic, ginger, oregano, paprika, rosemary and thyme. Turmeric is a powerful anti-inflammatory that will help your gut to heal.
* Celtic or Himalayan salt (but not refined iodized salt). You can add dulse flakes (a seaweed) to your salt for iodine and other essential trace minerals.
* additive-free coconut milk, coconut water and cold-pressed coconut oil products, which are satiating, soothing for the digestive tract and will promote the growth of healthy gut flora. Always look for coconut milk in BPA-free cans and without guar gum or citric acid.
* caffeine-free herbal teas. These are soothing for your tummy and are welcomed. Peppermint, spearmint, chamomile, lavender, rooibos, licorice root, dandelion root and other detoxifying blends are wonderful options. You can also drink Swiss-water-processed decaf caffe latte. Try the Curative Coffee recipe on page 136 – it's filling, and gut-restoring too!
* bone broths (see page 145), another highly important aspect of a gut-healing diet. Homemade chicken, beef, lamb or fish bone broths are

extremely mineral-rich and should be consumed daily. They're also high in naturally occurring gelatin, which is an incredibly powerful healer of the digestive lining. You can use this as a base for vegetable soups, or sip it throughout the day. Adding some slices of fresh ginger and a sprinkling of Celtic sea salt will provide a simple yet highly anti-inflammatory and mineral-rich afternoon cuppa.

* as many good fats as possible, to heal your gut and help deliver and draw out nutrients from your food, as well as remove from your body toxins and heavy metals such as aluminium, mercury, nickel and lead. Heavy metals can accumulate in your body and cause health issues. Eating good fats can cleanse the entire body as well as rebuild cell membranes. This is because these fats act as powerful antioxidants and they increase the production of bile by the liver, which eliminates heavy metals.

* flaxseed and fish oils, which are highly anti-inflammatory and will really help settle down your gut. The omega-3 component in fish is high in two fatty acids crucial to human health: eicosapentaenoic acid (EPA) and docosahexaenoic acid (DHA). Meat and eggs are also good sources of essential fatty acids.

* extra virgin coconut oil, extra virgin olive oil and ghee and butter, if you can tolerate them. Good fats act as carriers for important fat-soluble vitamins A, D, E and K, and for the conversion of beta-carotene to vitamin A.

GHEE WHIZZ! HEALING AND SEALING THE GUT BARRIER WITH GHEE

Used in Ayurvedic cooking, immunity-boosting ghee is a form of clarified butter that's especially good for lactose-intolerant people. It's a wonderful digestion aid and helps your body draw out and assimilate nutrients. Ghee will give you an energy boost, and the butyric acid it contains (a fatty acid) has antiviral properties. Ghee helps heal and seal the mucous lining of your digestive system by stimulating the secretion of stomach acids and balancing them out. It is a versatile fat that can be used in your recipes instead of butter, coconut or olive oil. When subbing for another oil, use half the amount stated in the recipe. Grass-fed ghee is best, and you'll love its sweet and nutty flavor.

SUPERCHARGED SWAP-OUTS

Next time you go shopping, switch on your "Are you for real?" radar in the back of your mind. It will really help you with your food choices.

It's easy to turn your recipes into real food recipes with just a few simple subs.

GOODBYE	HELLO
Margarine, hydrogenated fats, sunflower, vegetable, canola, soy, safflower and corn oils	Extra virgin olive oil and coconut oil, grass-fed organic butter, and fish and omega-3 oils
White refined flour, pre-packaged mixes, gluten flours, white rice, processed grains and pasta	Almond meal, gluten-free flours, buckwheat, quinoa, hazelnut, coconut, teff, arrowroot, tapioca and brown rice
Refined white sugar, corn syrup and artificial sweeteners	Stevia, rice malt syrup, coconut sugar, xylitol and raw honey
Table salt	Celtic sea salt, pink salt, Murray River salt and Himalayan salt
Guar gum, xanthan gum and cornstarch	Gluten-free baking powder, baking soda and arrowroot starch
Canned or pre-packaged stock, soups, sauces and vegetables	Homemade stock, soups and seasonal local vegetables
Irradiated herbs	Homegrown herbs
Low-fat anything	Anything full-fat, raw and organic

Befriend your body,
listen to what it's telling
you and learn to love its
inner wisdom.

Sip herbal tea. It's one excellent option for alleviating those sugar cravings.

CURBING CRAVINGS

A new health protocol brings with it a wave of excitement for reaching your future destination of healing and vitality, but it's really important to face the facts: an elemental diet won't always be a walk in the park. Ask any entrepreneur, visionary or high-level leader about achieving their success, and they'll always have a story of overcoming obstacles, opposition, doubts and failures. In making the decision to heal your gut, you too are in essence a leader – a leader of your own body and health.

Rather than succumbing to the health-opposing food culture around you, you're taking a stand for your own health, and committing to do whatever it takes to heal your gut and improve your life and long-term wellbeing. If you can allow this thought to keep your mindset strong during the elemental phase, you'll be one step ahead of people who go into a health protocol without an inner commitment.

One of the greatest obstacles you'll face in the beginning will be "the battle of the appetite." The shift from eating whatever your body craves to consuming only gut-healing and digestion-friendly foods will involve a sacrifice, and your body is likely to pull out the placards and protest.

Watching your friends and family blissfully munching down a Sunday lunch and dessert while you're slurping your healthy soups may arouse your appetite for other kinds of not-so-healthy-right-now foods. It's important to tell yourself that you're not the victim here, but rather that you're a *victor* who'll do whatever it takes to achieve healing and balanced health.

In moments like these, throughout the four-week protocol of phase one, you're going to need some armor. Although the appetite may be hardwired, you can do a number of practical things to kick those food cravings to the kerb.

* **SIP HERBAL TEA:** Licorice root tea has an amazing super-sweet taste that fills you with every sip, making it excellent during sugar cravings. Passing the time with a Nutmeg, Saffron and Cashew Nightcap (see page 132) or a Curative Coffee (see page 136) will make you feel nourished without sabotaging your healing and treatment protocol.
* **DO SOMETHING "SWEET" FOR YOURSELF:** If you're craving sugary foods, distract yourself by doing something that gives you that "sweet" feeling emotionally. Cuddle a loved one; take a long candlelit bath with Epsom salts (see page 75) and sweet-smelling essential oils; or, if you have a pet, snuggle up with them or take them out for a walk – anything that satisfies your craving emotionally rather than reaching for confectionery.
* **DISTRACT YOURSELF:** When the battle of the appetite rises, shift your mind to other things. Read one of your favorite books, get outside and go for a swim in the ocean (if you can) or take a nice walk in nature to get your endorphins pumping. Feeling a ray of sunshine on your skin will also improve your mood and help your cravings pass.
* **EAT REVERSE GATEWAY FOODS:** When "gateway foods" (foods that are particularly tempting) challenge you, fight back with a "reverse gateway food." Craving hot chips? Try some Cheesy Mashed Cauliflower (see page 206) instead. Deeply desiring sweets? Blend raspberries with some coconut water and freeze for a sugar-free sorbet, or enjoy some sweet mashed carrot and sweet potato to counteract your craving. Try Savory Smashed Root Vegetables (see page 227) or some Scrambled Eggs (see page 218).
* **KEEP BUSY:** Have you ever noticed that when you're really busy, you don't think about food as much? Pull out your calendar and fill it up with goals and tasks, particularly ones you're passionate about and that make you feel inspired and engaged.
* **EAT REGULARLY AND MINDFULLY:** Cravings are less likely to occur if you have your meals regularly throughout the day. Be mindful of the goodness that's filling your body and thankful that you're now healing your gut. These positive thoughts will keep you focused and on track.

SUPERCHARGED TIP

Keep busy doing the things you love to do. Boredom is the ultimate appetite increasing agent.

MAINTENANCE ON THE FLY

It's relatively easy to stay on the gut-healing protocol when you're in the comfort of your own home, but real life can sometimes throw a wrench in the works. The demands of your work life, a busy family schedule, work-related travel and vacations can leave you with minimal control over what you put into your body. Rather than letting outside circumstances unravel all your efforts while healing your gut, here are a few strategies you can put in place for maintaining your healing on the fly.

MAKE A MEAL PLAN

Following a meal plan makes life significantly less chaotic. By organizing your week's worth of meals in advance you'll never be left in a situation where you're stuck for something to eat, and you'll be much less likely to reach for a gut-sabotaging snack. All you need is an hour each week where you can sit down and design your meal plan and correlating shopping list with appropriate ingredients. There are even set meal planners you can use in this book if you don't want to create your own. Remember, whatever phase of the gut-healing protocol you're on, you can plan your meals ahead for the coming week. My favorite meal-planning days are Sundays, as they're the most convenient for me, but perhaps for you it could be midweek or even a free weekend night.

FIX AND FREEZE YOUR MAKE-AHEADS

The beauty of my gut-healing recipes is that they're fridge and freezer friendly, particularly the soups, stocks and smoothies, and they taste even better the next day. Once your meal planning and shopping are complete for the week ahead, it's time to start creating your grab-and-go meals. I recommend cooking up large batches of recipes such as Fennel, Tomato and Roast Garlic Soup (see page 184), Parsley and Leek Soup with Lemon (see page 198) or Pea, Spinach and Lamb Soup (see page 154), and dividing these into single-serve portions so you can transport them to work easily. Try to use this day to have all your time-consuming meal preparations done: chopping, washing and cooking veggies and blending can all be done in advance. Then fill your freezer and fridge with your homemade convenience foods made your way.

SUPERCHARGED TIP

Take an avocado to work and make an instant mash with a drizzle of lemon or lime and some freshly cracked pepper. Add a couple of dashes of wheat-free tamari and apple cider vinegar. It's my favorite in-a-pinch snack, full of appropriately healthy anti-inflammatory fats.

PREPARE GOOD FOOD FOR WHEN YOU'RE ON THE GO

Make up "dry mixes" and seal them in zip-lock bags. You can also prepare all of the dry ingredients included in the herbal tea mixtures, such as the Anti-inflammatory Toddy (see page 128), Aromatic Curry Leaf Tisane (see page 131) and Dandy Chai Latte (see page 143) in advance and in bulk by using dried spices and powdered stevia. Take them to work in zip-lock bags, then just pour into a cup and add hot water. Dry mixes are also my secret weapon during flights. Strict airport laws unfortunately prevent the carrying of liquids, but you can carry a pre-made dry mix and ask for water on the plane, or find other liquid ingredients at your destination. Dry mixtures of my Supercharged Shake (see page 104) are also a terrific way to fuel yourself conveniently while on vacations, and give yourself a boost of nutrients. Zip-lock bags are useful because they mold to any shape and you can pop them in your carry-on luggage.

Invest in a thermos. A good stainless-steel spill-proof thermos can be easily filled with fiber-rich soups, hot drinks and mashes on the go. Insulated thermoses can keep food warm for up to seven hours. Choose a thermos with a wide mouth so that you can easily dig a spoon into it instead of using a bowl, to save on washing dishes. Or you could buy one with a cap that doubles as a bowl. Fold a tea towel and wrap it around the bottom of your thermos to help maintain the temperature. It also doubles as a napkin! Keeping a small plunger at work will allow you to enjoy your "dry mix" teas easily, sans tea bag.

Seek out old jars to use as wonderful, affordable, BPA- and chemical-free smoothie, salad, soup, and just-about-anything transporters. If you're carrying it in your bag, wrap it in a scarf or tea towel to keep it secure and snug. If you're looking for a foolproof and leak-proof solution, try canning jars. They're rugged and durable and made from thicker glass, making them more jostle-proof! Mason jars with no-leak lids can be fitted and rugged up with a homemade washable cover to keep them insulated and avoid spillage. Containers with screw-top lids are also handy for packing liquids safely. Jars give food less of a leftover feel and more of a homemade impression. Bring your own cutlery for a waste-free meal.

The key to successful gut healing is to be organized, with convenient, ready-to-go meals in your gut-healing arsenal. Heat up soups on the stovetop wherever possible, as the microwave will kill nutrients and turn them into toxic compounds. You're better off consuming soups at room temperature than from the microwave.

SUPERCHARGED TIP

Before adding hot soup to your thermos, pour in some warm water and swish it around, then pour it out. Add your piping hot soup and close the lid immediately. This will help keep your soup as warm as possible. Second law of thermodynamics!

STOCK UP YOUR WORKPLACE

If you have access to a fridge and kitchenette space at work, fill it with anything you know you'll need. Stock up on almond and coconut milk for tea and supplement powders, any fresh raw ingredients such as avocados to mash and smash over soups, and berries to top off smoothies. Label and date these ingredients to ensure they're clearly defined and won't be thrown out or eaten by accident. Upgrade your midday meal by keeping a beautiful bowl, glass, mug and cutlery at work, and make me a pinky promise never to eat out of a plastic container again. Try to have lunch outside and avoid "lunch al desko" – your mind and body will both say thank you.

TASTY TOPPERS

Time to stock up your desk drawers with delicious and belly-friendly toppers. These additions will take your lunch-bowl go-to from satisfactory to satisfying.

* **NUTRITIONAL YEAST FLAKES:** A sprinkling of cheesy-flavored nutritional yeast will move you one step closer to creating the lunch bowl of your dreams. These bright mustard-yellow flakes make a fantastic natural flavor enhancer. Loaded with B vitamins (a little less than 1 tablespoon supplies the adult recommended daily intake of vitamin B12), amino acids and minerals, they can be used in cooking, as a condiment or warm beverage. Because the yeast is no longer living, it does not feed candida and so is safe for your gut. They can be purchased from health food stores or online.
* **CELTIC SEA SALT:** Bring in a mini-pot of sea salt to scatter onto soups. Many sea salt brands come in portable containers.
* **APPLE CIDER VINEGAR:** This will punch up your soups for that just-off-the-stovetop feeling.
* **EXTRA VIRGIN OLIVE OIL:** Drizzle on soups for an extra boost of anti-inflammatory gut-healing fats.
* **WHEAT-FREE TAMARI:** Add a dash of naturally fermented wheat-free tamari as a natural flavor enhancer for soups and mashes.
* **DULSE FLAKES:** Think of them as sprinkles of fiber-rich goodness. Shake this mellow sea vegetable over mashes or soups for an extra layer of seasoning.
* **CRACKED PEPPER:** Grind bold flavors onto your lunch bowl and wave goodbye to tasteless paper pepper packets.

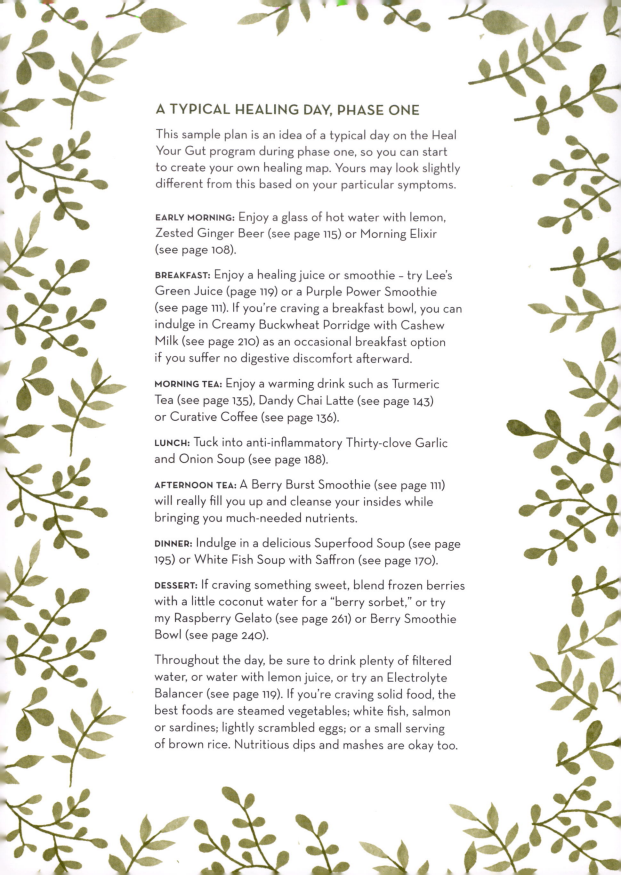

A TYPICAL HEALING DAY, PHASE ONE

This sample plan is an idea of a typical day on the Heal Your Gut program during phase one, so you can start to create your own healing map. Yours may look slightly different from this based on your particular symptoms.

EARLY MORNING: Enjoy a glass of hot water with lemon, Zested Ginger Beer (see page 115) or Morning Elixir (see page 108).

BREAKFAST: Enjoy a healing juice or smoothie – try Lee's Green Juice (page 119) or a Purple Power Smoothie (see page 111). If you're craving a breakfast bowl, you can indulge in Creamy Buckwheat Porridge with Cashew Milk (see page 210) as an occasional breakfast option if you suffer no digestive discomfort afterward.

MORNING TEA: Enjoy a warming drink such as Turmeric Tea (see page 135), Dandy Chai Latte (see page 143) or Curative Coffee (see page 136).

LUNCH: Tuck into anti-inflammatory Thirty-clove Garlic and Onion Soup (see page 188).

AFTERNOON TEA: A Berry Burst Smoothie (see page 111) will really fill you up and cleanse your insides while bringing you much-needed nutrients.

DINNER: Indulge in a delicious Superfood Soup (see page 195) or White Fish Soup with Saffron (see page 170).

DESSERT: If craving something sweet, blend frozen berries with a little coconut water for a "berry sorbet," or try my Raspberry Gelato (see page 261) or Berry Smoothie Bowl (see page 240).

Throughout the day, be sure to drink plenty of filtered water, or water with lemon juice, or try an Electrolyte Balancer (see page 119). If you're craving solid food, the best foods are steamed vegetables; white fish, salmon or sardines; lightly scrambled eggs; or a small serving of brown rice. Nutritious dips and mashes are okay too.

Here are some more ideas to inspire your menu planning for phase one, the initial four-week period.

BREAKFAST: Try juices or smoothies made with avocado, cucumber, lemon, lime, spinach, kale, zucchini, broccoli, fennel, cilantro or parsley. Mix up the flavors!

SNACKS: Drink Soothing Sage, Mint and Ginger Tea (see page 140), homemade bone broth (see page 145), homemade vegetable stock (see page 151), or green smoothies blended with coconut water or coconut milk. Avocados and a spoonful of coconut oil blended into a smoothie will make it creamy and filling. You can have a smash or mash bowl if you feel the need for a hearty snack (see "Easy-to-digest meals in a bowl" on page 205).

LUNCH OR DINNER: Enjoy Lemongrass Thai Soup (see page 178), Lamb and Zucchini Soup (see page 196), Karmic Korma (see page 176) or any other soup made from sautéed, steamed or roasted vegetables, combined with herbs, spices and Celtic or Himalayan sea salt. Blend with bone broth, vegetable stock or filtered water. For a creamier soup, add coconut milk. If you're feeling fishy, chow down on Salmon Chowder (see page 187) or indulge in a fun Sardine Mash Pot (see page 217).

CREATING YOUR OWN HEALING PLAN

Now that you have the information you need to start your four-week protocol, it's time to look through the recipes and choose your favorites, then create your own healing plan.

Start by flipping over to "Your personal planner" (see page 66) and creating your own based on the information I've given you, or use the weekly planners on the following pages as a guide. These include my own personal planner plus a vegetarian version and a planner for busy people. I've also included a planner for daily restorative activities.

Once you've decided which recipes you're going to incorporate into your four-week protocol, you can start to pull together your shopping list using the basic lists on pages 100–101.

TIPS FOR JUICING

Juicing and making smoothies is a big part of the four-week protocol, especially at breakfast time or afternoon tea, when you feel like an easy and nutritious high-fiber tummy-filler. Let's face it, who wants to gnaw their way through a raw salad first thing in the morning?

Blending your vegetables makes mornings more convenient, and it's a great way to give your belly a rest and boost the bioavailability of incoming nutrients. Having a morning smoothie has so many health benefits, from boosting your immune system to helping balance your hormones. My daily smoothie is delicious and consists of spinach, kale, celery, cucumber, mint, ginger and coconut water. To make things more efficient, I prepare and chop my ingredients on the weekend and place them in containers in the fridge. Try to source fresh organic, locally grown veggies if you can, to lower your pesticide intake.

When it comes to green vegetables, it doesn't take a rocket scientist to figure out they're good for you. But turn the clock back to high school science class, and you may recall that green vegetables are overflowing with chlorophyll. This green guru helps detoxify the body of heavy metals, improve circulation, oxygenate the blood and fight infection. Vegetables are also highly alkalizing. A highly acidic environment is where illness will be in its element, so pump up your produce and keep your body's acid and alkaline levels balanced.

In a nutshell, here are four good reasons to choose green vegetables when it comes to juices and smoothies, particularly when you have an overtaxed digestive system and you're healing your gut:

1. They're a major detoxifier and internal cleanser.
2. They help alkalize the body.
3. They support and strengthen the immune system.
4. They provide the body with energy.

SEVEN DAYS OF SOOTHING SOUPS

4

5

6

7

WEEKLY MEAL PLANNER WEEK 1

These plans are just a guide to show you the variety of recipes available. You might want to have the same meal a couple of days in a row if you've made extra quantities.

If you're still hungry after a soup, try one of the "Easy-to-digest meals in a bowl" (see page 205). It's best to avoid starchy vegetables such as yams, potatoes, pumpkin (squash), sweet potato, parsnips and carrots in the first four weeks, but tuck into Savoury Smashed Root Vegetables (see page 227) if you feel like something sweet. It won't delay your progress and it will help you overcome the craving.

	MONDAY	TUESDAY	WEDNESDAY
AFTER RISING	Morning Elixir (108)	Electrolyte Balancer (119)	Aromatic Curry Leaf Tisane (131)
BREAKFAST	Berry Burst Smoothie (111)	Overnight Edible Smoothie (116)	Scrambled Eggs (218)
MID-MORNING	Curative Coffee (136)	Dandy Chai Latte (143)	Curative Coffee (136)
LUNCH	Broccolini, Kale and Mint Soup (199)	Pea, Spinach and Lamb Soup (154) + Cumin Digestive Aid (107)	Super-quick Chicken Soup (183)
DINNER	Salmon Chowder (187) + Broccoli Mash (225)	Market-fresh Vegetable Soup (158) + Ratatouille Bowl (213)	Sweet Green Bean Soup (164) + Savory Smashed Root Vegetables (227)
DESSERT	Vanilla Custard (245) + Nutmeg, Saffron and Cashew Nightcap (132)	Berry Smoothie Bowl (240) + Soothing Sage, Mint and Ginger Tea (140)	Almond Milk Jelly Cup (250) + Anti-inflammatory Toddy (128)

Berries are the fruit least likely to cause digestive problems and can be eaten in moderation. If they cause an increase in symptoms for you, avoid them altogether for four weeks then reintroduce them once your gut is healed and your symptoms have subsided.

If you're following a low-FODMAP diet for food intolerances, replace the onion and garlic in recipes with the green part of a scallion, or with chives or asafoetida.

If coconut milk is a problem for you, use nut or seed milks instead.

NOTE: *Numbers in brackets are page numbers for recipes. An asterisk (*) means optional.*

THURSDAY	FRIDAY	SATURDAY	SUNDAY
Zested Ginger Beer (115)	Morning Elixir (108)	Chicken Broth (146)	Anti-inflammatory Toddy (128)
Lee's Green Juice (119)	Creamy Buckwheat Porridge with Cashew Milk (210)	Squashy Yellow Squash (221)	Chicken Broth (146)
Choc Mint Hot Chocolate (136)	Dandy Chai Latte (143)	Spiced Almond Chai (139)	Turmeric Tea (135)
Bok Choy and Mushroom Soup (181)	Superfood Soup (195)	Parsley and Leek Soup with Lemon (198)	White Fish Soup with Saffron (170)
Celery Leek and Thyme Soup (169) + Cheesy Mashed Cauliflower (206)	Cheesy Mashed Cauliflower (206) + Mushy Peas (214) + Cumin Digestive Aid (107)	Lemongrass Thai Soup (178) + Squashy Yellow Squash (221)	Grandma's Chicken Soup (157) + Green Bean, Tomato and Mint Mash (222)
Tapioca Pudding (241) + Chamomile and Lavender Tea (135)	Raspberry Gelato (261) + Soothing Sage, Mint and Ginger Tea (140)	Baked Blueberry Custards (262) + Nutmeg, Saffron and Cashew Nightcap (132)	Chai Custard (245) + Chamomile and Lavender Tea (135)

WEEKLY MEAL PLANNER WEEK 2

	MONDAY	TUESDAY	WEDNESDAY
AFTER RISING	Morning Elixir (108)	Electrolyte Balancer (119)	Hot water with lemon and apple cider vinegar
BREAKFAST	Cheesy Mashed Cauliflower (206)	Creamy Buckwheat Porridge with Cashew Milk (210)	Scrambled Eggs (218) with avocado
MID-MORNING	Spiced Almond Chai (139)	Turmeric Tea (135)	Curative Coffee (136)
LUNCH	Zesty Zucchini Soup (203)	Summer Herb Soup (172) or Grandma's Chicken Soup (157)	Fennel, Tomato and Roast Garlic Soup (184) + Cumin Digestive Aid (107)
DINNER	Pea, Spinach and Lamb Soup (154) + Salmon and Broccoli Bowl (209)	Iceberg Lettuce and Coconut Soup (175) + Sardine Mash Pot (217)	Creamy Mushroom Soup (191) + Cheesy Mashed Cauliflower (206)
DESSERT	Avocado Ice Cream (258) + Soothing Sage, Mint and Ginger Tea (140)	Tapioca Pudding (241) + Anti-inflammatory Toddy (128)	Anti-inflammatory Squash Whip (242) + Dandy Chai Latte (143)

THURSDAY	FRIDAY	SATURDAY	SUNDAY
Chamomile and Lavender Tea (135)	Zested Ginger Beer (115)	Vegetable Stock (151)	Cleanse and Renew Smoothie (104)
Berry Burst Smoothie (111)	Overnight Edible Smoothie (116)	Creamy Buckwheat Porridge with Cashew Milk (210)	Scrambled Eggs (218) + Mushy Peas (214)
Anti-inflammatory Toddy (128)	Dandy Chai Latte (143)	Turmeric Tea (135)	Choc Mint Hot Chocolate (136)
Salmon Chowder (187)	Sweet Green Bean Soup (164) + Squashy Yellow Squash (221)	Delectable Detox Soup (182)	Pea, Spinach and Lamb Soup (154) + Cumin Digestive Aid (107)
Garden-fresh Asparagus Soup (201) + Green Bean, Tomato and Mint Mash (222)	White Fish Soup with Saffron (170) + Salmon and Broccoli Bowl (209)	Sweet Green Bean Soup (164) + Squashy Yellow Squash (221) + Mushy Peas (214)	Karmic Korma (176) + Minty Smashed Zucchini with Garlic (226)
Chocolaty Mousse (254) + Nutmeg, Saffron and Cashew Nightcap (132)	Raspberry and Lime Pudding (261) + Spiced Almond Chai (139)	Chai Custard (245) + Anti-inflammatory Toddy (128)	Baked Blueberry Custards (262) + Nutmeg, Saffron and Cashew Nightcap (132)

	MONDAY	TUESDAY	WEDNESDAY
AFTER RISING	Hot water with lemon and apple cider vinegar	Zested Ginger Beer (115) or Homemade Kombucha (236) with ginger	Cleanse and Renew Smoothie (104)
BREAKFAST	Creamy Buckwheat Porridge with Cashew Milk (210)	Scrambled Eggs (218) + Squashy Yellow Squash (221) + Fermented Salsa* (235)	Salmon and Broccoli Bowl (209) + Cultured Vegetables* (230)
MID-MORNING	Curative Coffee (136)	Spiced Almond Chai (139)	Dandy Chai Latte (143)
LUNCH	Zesty Zucchini Soup (203) + Easy-to-make Sauerkraut* (233)	Pea, Spinach and Lamb Soup (154) + Squashy Yellow Squash (221)	Fennel, Tomato and Roast Garlic Soup (184) + Broccoli Mash (225) + Cumin Digestive Aid (107)
DINNER	Iceberg Lettuce and Coconut Soup (175) + Savory Smashed Root Vegetables (227)	Summer Herb Soup (172) + Easy-to-make Sauerkraut* (233)	Watercress, Leek and Coconut Soup (167) + Minty Smashed Zucchini with Garlic (226)
DESSERT	Vanilla Custard (245) + Nutmeg, Saffron and Cashew Nightcap (132)	Berry Smoothie Bowl (240) + Soothing Sage, Mint and Ginger Tea (140)	Almond Milk Jelly Cup (250) + Anti-inflammatory Toddy (128)

THURSDAY	FRIDAY	SATURDAY	SUNDAY
Vegetable Stock (151)	Electrolyte Balancer (119) or Homemade Kombucha (236)	Hot water with lemon and apple cider vinegar	Morning Elixir (108) or Homemade Kombucha (236)
Ratatouille Bowl (213) + Kimchi* (232)	Overnight Edible Smoothie (116)	Berry Smoothie Bowl (240)	Creamy Buckwheat Porridge with Cashew Milk (210)
Choc Mint Hot Chocolate (136)	Anti-inflammatory Toddy (128)	Curative Coffee (136)	Spiced Almond Chai (139)
Salmon Chowder (187) + Cultured Vegetables* (230)	Sweet Green Bean Soup (164) + Cheesy Mashed Cauliflower (206) + Mushy Peas (214)	Delectable Detox Soup (182) + Cultured Vegetables* (230)	Summer Herb Soup (172) + Cumin Digestive Aid (107)
Thirty-clove Garlic and Onion Soup (188) or Karmic Korma (176) + Kimchi* (232)	Avocado and Almond Soup (163) + Salmon and Broccoli Bowl (209)	Comforting Cauli and Turnip Soup (194) + Green Bean, Tomato and Mint Mash (222)	Grandma's Chicken Soup (157) + Squashy Yellow Squash (221)
Tapioca Pudding (241) + Chamomile and Lavender Tea (135)	Raspberry Gelato (261) + Soothing Sage, Mint and Ginger Tea (140)	Baked Blueberry Custards (262) + Nutmeg, Saffron and Cashew Nightcap (132)	Chai Custard (245) + Chamomile and Lavender Tea (135)

	MONDAY	TUESDAY	WEDNESDAY
AFTER RISING	Homemade Kombucha (236) with ginger	Vegetable Stock (151)	Cleanse and Renew Smoothie (104)
BREAKFAST	Berry Smoothie Bowl (240)	Salmon and Broccoli Bowl (209) + Cultured Vegetables* (230)	Creamy Buckwheat Porridge with Cashew Milk (210)
MID-MORNING	Spiced Almond Chai (139)	Curative Coffee (136)	Choc Mint Hot Chocolate (136)
LUNCH	Pea, Spinach and Lamb Soup (154) + Cumin Digestive Aid (107)	Super-quick Chicken Soup (183) + Broccoli Mash (225) + Easy-to-make Sauerkraut* (233)	Bok Choy and Mushroom Soup (181) + Cumin Digestive Aid (107)
DINNER	Lemongrass Thai Soup (178) + Squashy Yellow Squash (221) + Easy-to-make Sauerkraut* (233)	Iceberg Lettuce and Coconut Soup (175) + Savory Smashed Root Vegetables (227)	Celery, Leek and Thyme Soup (169) + Cheesy Mashed Cauliflower (206)
DESSERT	Avocado Ice Cream (258) + Dandy Chai Latte (143)	Kefir Yogurt (253) + Spiced Almond Chai (139)	Baked Blueberry Custards (262) + Nutmeg, Saffron and Cashew Nightcap (132)

THURSDAY	FRIDAY	SATURDAY	SUNDAY
Hot water with lemon and apple cider vinegar	Zested Ginger Beer (115)	Morning Elixir (108)	Homemade Kombucha (236) with ginger
Ratatouille Bowl (213) + Kimchi* (232)	Scrambled Eggs (218) + Squashy Yellow Squash (221) and Kimchi* (232)	Berry Smoothie Bowl (240)	Creamy Buckwheat Porridge with Cashew Milk (210)
Anti-inflammatory Toddy (128)	Curative Coffee (136)	Anti-inflammatory Toddy (128)	Dandy Chai Latte (143)
Sweet Green Bean Soup (164) + Cultured Vegetables* (230)	Parsley and Leek Soup with Lemon (198) + Cheesy Mashed Cauliflower (206) + Mushy Peas (214) + Cumin Digestive Aid (107)	Fennel, Tomato and Roast Garlic Soup (184) + Cultured Vegetables* (230)	Salmon Chowder (187) + Cultured Vegetables* (230)
Market-fresh Vegetable Soup (158) + Ratatouille Bowl (213) + Kimchi* (232)	Salmon Chowder (187) + Squashy Yellow Squash (221)	White Fish Soup with Saffron (170) + Green Bean, Tomato and Mint Mash (222)	Grandma's Chicken Soup (157) + Broccoli Mash (225)
Berry Smoothie Bowl (240) + Soothing Sage, Mint and Ginger Tea (140)	Kefir Yogurt (253) + Turmeric Tea (135)	Raspberry and Lime Pudding (261) + Nutmeg, Saffron and Cashew Nightcap (132)	Tapioca Pudding (241) + Choc Mint Hot Chocolate (136)

VEGETARIAN WEEKLY MEAL PLANNER

To increase your protein intake during the elemental diet, try these options:

* Add ¼ cup (1¾ oz/50 g) quinoa to soups, for adequate protein (¼ oz per cup/8 g) and nine essential amino acids.
* Choose protein-rich vegetables, such as green peas (¼ oz protein per cup/7.9 g), broccoli (¼ oz per cup/8 g), artichokes (⅛ oz per cup/6 g) and leafy greens.
* Add spirulina powder to smoothies. Spirulina is one of the best-known protein sources (70 percent complete protein versus cooked steak at 25 percent).
* Use nut milk in smoothies: almond, cashew and pistachio milk are highest in protein.
* If your tummy can handle them, add a sprinkle of chia seeds to desserts for ⅛ oz/5 g protein per 2 tablespoons.

	MONDAY	TUESDAY	WEDNESDAY
AFTER RISING	Morning Elixir (108)	Electrolyte Balancer (119)	Aromatic Curry Leaf Tisane (131)
BREAKFAST	Avocado Lassi (112)	Minty Smashed Zucchini with Garlic (226)	Creamy Buckwheat Porridge with Cashew Milk (210)
MID-MORNING	Spiced Almond Chai (139)	Dandy Chai Latte (143)	Anti-inflammatory Toddy (128)
LUNCH	Anti-inflammatory Cauli Soup (161)	Zesty Zucchini Soup (203) + Cumin Digestive Aid (107)	Iceberg Lettuce and Coconut Soup (175)
DINNER	Flirty French Onion Soup (192) + Cheesy Mashed Cauliflower (206)	Market-fresh Vegetable Soup (158) + Ratatouille Bowl (213)	Sweet Green Bean Soup (164) + Savory Smashed Root Vegetables (227)
DESSERT	Berry Smoothie Bowl (240) + Soothing Sage, Mint and Ginger Tea (140)	Nutmeg, Saffron and Cashew Nightcap (132)	Chocolaty Mousse (254) + Turmeric Tea (135)

* Add hemp powder (¼ oz protein/10 g per ¼ cup) to smoothies.
* Make the Chocolaty Mousse (page 254). Cacao does contain caffeine, so eat it only in moderation while healing your gut, and earlier in the day is best.
* If you're not vegan, try sprinkling bee pollen on top of smoothies, porridge or desserts for a healthy protein boost.
* If you can tolerate them without candida symptoms, after the first couple of weeks, add high-protein lentils, chickpeas, white beans or pinto beans to soups with ¼ cup (1¾ oz/50 g) quinoa. Soak them overnight and rinse them well so they're easier to digest. Adding kombu to the cooking water makes them easier on the tummy and makes their nutrients more bioavailable.
* Add nutritional yeast.

THURSDAY	FRIDAY	SATURDAY	SUNDAY
Zested Ginger Beer (115)	Hot water with lemon and apple cider vinegar	Vegetable Stock (151)	Anti-inflammatory Toddy (128)
Overnight Edible Smoothie (116)	Berry Burst Smoothie (111)	Green Bean, Tomato and Mint Mash (222)	Ratatouille Bowl (213)
Choc Mint Hot Chocolate (136)	Dandy Chai Latte (143)	Spiced Almond Chai (139)	Turmeric Tea (135)
Bok Choy and Mushroom Soup (181)	Superfood Soup (195)	Parsley and Leek Soup with Lemon (198)	Karmic Korma (176)
Summer Herb Soup (172) + Minty Smashed Zucchini with Garlic (226)	Fennel, Tomato and Roast Garlic Soup (184) + Cheesy Mashed Cauliflower (206)	Lemongrass Thai Soup (178) + Squashy Yellow Squash (221) + Ratatouille Bowl (213)	Broccolini, Kale and Mint Soup (199) + Green Bean, Tomato and Mint Mash (222)
Avocado Ice Cream (258) + Soothing Sage, Mint and Ginger Tea (140)	Raspberry Gelato (261) + Chamomile and Lavender Tea (135)	Nutmeg, Saffron and Cashew Nightcap (132)	Avocado Ice Cream (258) + Chamomile and Lavender Tea (135)

WEEKLY MEAL PLANNER FOR BUSY PEOPLE

	MONDAY	TUESDAY	WEDNESDAY
AFTER RISING	Hot water with lemon and apple cider vinegar	Electrolyte Balancer (119)	Morning Elixir (108)
BREAKFAST	Creamy Buckwheat Porridge with Cashew Milk (210)	Scrambled Eggs (218)	Berry Smoothie Bowl (240)
MID-MORNING	Dandy Chai Latte (143)	Ratatouille Bowl (213)	Curative Coffee (136)
LUNCH	Lamb and Zucchini Soup (196)	Superfood Soup (195)	Lamb and Zucchini Soup (196)
DINNER	Superfood Soup (195)	Lamb and Zucchini Soup (196) + Ratatouille Bowl (213)	Superfood Soup (195) + Cheesy Mashed Cauliflower (206)
DESSERT	Almond Milk Jelly Cup (250)	Avocado Ice Cream (258)	Vanilla Custard (245)

THURSDAY	FRIDAY	SATURDAY	SUNDAY
Hot water with lemon and apple cider vinegar	Electrolyte Balancer (119) + Chicken Broth (146)	Hot water with lemon and apple cider vinegar	Morning Elixir (108)
Green Bean, Tomato and Mint Mash (222)	Sardine Mash Pot (217)	Scrambled Eggs (218)	Salmon and Broccoli Bowl (209)
Dandy Chai Latte (143)	Soothing Sage, Mint and Ginger Tea (140)	Chicken Broth (146)	Anti-inflammatory Toddy (128)
White Fish Soup with Saffron (170) + Green Bean, Tomato and Mint Mash (222)	Pea, Spinach and Lamb Soup (154)	Broccolini, Kale and Mint Soup (199)	Pea, Spinach and Lamb Soup (154) + Salmon and Broccoli Bowl (209)
Broccoli, Kale and Mint Soup (199)	White Fish Soup with Saffron (170) + Sardine Mash Pot (217)	Pea, Spinach and Lamb Soup (154)	Salmon Chowder (187) + Cumin Digestive Aid (107)
Avocado Ice Cream (258)	Chai Custard (245)	Smashed Raspberry (257)	Raspberry and Lime Pudding (261)

DAILY RESTORATIVE ACTIVITIES PLANNER

	WEEKDAYS	WEEKENDS
SPIRITUAL PRACTICE AND MEDITATION	Spend 10 minutes breathing into your belly (deeply, from your diaphragm) each morning before work	Spend 10 minutes breathing into your belly (deeply, from your diaphragm) each morning
EXERCISE AND MOVEMENT	Take a 10-minute walk around the block at lunchtime every other day	Do some gentle stretching each day
SLEEP	Go to bed before 10 pm each day Have an Epsom salts bath (see page 75) before bed and do some guided meditation before sleep every other day	

YOUR PERSONAL PLANNER

	MONDAY	TUESDAY	WEDNESDAY
AFTER RISING			
BREAKFAST			
MID-MORNING			
LUNCH			
DINNER			
DESSERT			
SPIRITUAL PRACTICE AND MEDITATION			
EXERCISE AND MOVEMENT			
SLEEP			

THURSDAY	FRIDAY	SATURDAY	SUNDAY

DETOX YOUR BODY

CLEANSE AND SWEEP

As your gut lining starts to heal you can begin to detox your body further. Remember that during the four-week elemental diet you're still detoxing your body through the foods you're eating, particularly if you're also having adequate amounts of water. You can start further detoxing on week two of the four-week protocol if you feel up to it, or wait until you feel ready. The elemental diet also detoxifies the body, so you don't have to be concerned that you're not doing all you can – small steps are better than big ones. It's taken years for your condition to arise, so healing, especially natural healing, takes time, and having patience is important. Another factor in waiting to start phase two at least two weeks into the four-week elemental diet is that once you've improved your digestion, this will greatly improve your detoxification capabilities.

The increase of symptoms we feel when embarking on a detox program is often known as a detox reaction or a Herxheimer reaction. These reactions occur when the body tries to eliminate toxins at a faster rate than they can be properly disposed of. Often you may feel worse, with additional flu-like symptoms and headaches, and conclude that the treatment isn't working. Yet these reactions are in fact signs that your body is beginning the process of cleansing itself of impurities, toxins and imbalances. The increased reactions are temporary and can occur immediately or within several days or weeks. In some cases, the symptoms can be identical to the health issues you may be experiencing, so it can be really confusing.

The type of detox reaction you'll experience will depend on your level of health or the severity of your present health condition. As old bacteria die off and are replaced by new healthy tissue, the toxins within the bacteria (endotoxins) are released into the body. The more severe the initial state of your body, the more bacteria are present. With larger quantities of bacteria come an increased number of endotoxins and hence a stronger cleansing reaction. This is when it's really important to rest and try to help the detox process along.

STAYING HYDRATED

A very simple method for avoiding or decreasing detox reactions is to ensure adequate hydration and mineral consumption. It's important to drink as much water as possible, to flush the toxins from your body. Having your daily green juice will provide essential nutrients that your body can absorb easily.

Another hydrator and detoxer to include in your morning routine is lemon juice in warm water. It's a good digestive aid and can alleviate symptoms of indigestion, stomach pain and bloating because the bowels are aided in eliminating waste more efficiently, thus controlling constipation and diarrhea. Lemon has strong antibacterial, antiviral and immune-boosting powers, and is an effective liver cleanser. Lemons contain natural citric acid, calcium, magnesium, copper, folic acid, iron, vitamin B6, vitamin C and bioflavonoids to promote immunity and fight infection; the juice also makes a useful gargle for sore throats and mouth ulcers. They are a very good source of dietary fiber, which helps promote good gut bacteria. Make sure you're including your daily warm water and lemon to help the detox process along. To stimulate your adrenal glands, you can add a pinch of Celtic sea salt to your morning drink.

HOW TO MAKE LEMON JUICE IN WARM WATER

Fill the kettle with filtered water, boil, then allow it to cool to a comfortable warmth. Squeeze half a fresh lemon (or pour 3 tablespoons (60 ml) freshly squeezed additive-free juice) into a cup or heat-resistant glass and add the water. Wait 20–30 minutes before consuming. Drink first thing in the morning. Some people like to drink it through a straw as the acid in lemon can affect your tooth enamel. If you're out and about, most eateries and cafés will be able to accommodate you if you ask for hot water and lemon.

DRY SKIN BRUSHING

Before you embark on your morning shower or bath, spend a few minutes practicing dry skin brushing. This mainstay of the Ayurvedic way of life helps you detox and excrete impurities through your skin – the largest and most important eliminative organ. Your skin is usually the last organ to benefit from nutrients in the body, yet it's the first to show signs of an imbalance or deficiency. Dry skin brushing activates the lymphatic system by aiding the flow of lymph through the body. It stimulates the liver and adrenal glands, helping them decongest and dump their toxins.

Dry skin brushing has many benefits. It:

* aids digestion and kidney function
* promotes cell renewal and rejuvenation
* encourages your body to discharge metabolic wastes
* stimulates acupressure points
* helps your skin absorb nutrients
* strengthens the immune system
* promotes muscle tone and even distribution of fat deposits
* removes dead skin cells and outer impurities
* stimulates and increases blood circulation
* assists the eliminative capacity of your body's organs.

STEP-BY-STEP GUIDE TO DRY SKIN BRUSHING

Invest in a long-handled bath brush with natural bristles (not synthetic ones, which can damage the skin and be harsh and irritating). The brush needs to be kept dry and should pass once over every part of your body except your face. Use long strokes – there's no need to scrub – and go back and forth in a circular motion. You should only brush toward the heart. To keep the brush fresh, wash it with soap and water every couple of weeks and let it dry naturally. A loofah can also be used.

1   Brush first thing in the morning before your shower. Ensure your skin and the brush are completely dry.
2   Begin with the soles of your feet, then work upwards on both sides of your legs. Next brush your back, then around to your abdomen, working clockwise, following the direction of your colon. Then head up toward your heart, being careful with the chest region.
3   Avoid brushing your face, as it's a sensitive region.
4   Use gentle strokes to start with, so that you can get used to the sensation. Your skin should be stimulated and slightly tingly, but not irritated or red.
5   Have a shower to remove debris and dead skin cells.

HOW TO REST INTENTIONALLY

Find a quiet place to make your meditation session special.
Sit in a comfortable position or lie down, and start by
focusing on the area of your body that's causing you anxiety,
discomfort, pain or inflammation. You'll notice that when
you bring your awareness and attention to that part of your
body or mind, your body will tense up automatically. That's
how we're accustomed to dealing with pain. Breathe for a
moment into your belly (taking deep breaths to the bottom
of your lungs by engaging your diaphragm) and focus on your
breath, imagining you're truly resting the part of your body
that's in pain. Don't try to fix it, just focus on letting it rest
intentionally.

Do this exercise anywhere and whenever you're in pain. It will
allow you to truly rest and restore energy to that area. Bingo!

SET YOUR INTENTION

Before we begin, let's get into the right headspace and set an intention
to truly promote healing. Remember, stress is one of the factors
leading to an unhappy gut, so try to lessen any stressors you may
currently have in your life. It's also time to embrace your intuition and
start to flex your "Mr or Mrs No" muscle. That might mean saying no to
people or invitations, and placing your people-pleaser tendencies on
the back burner both personally and professionally.

It's time for a dose of self-care and nourishment so that you can
preserve your most valuable resource: you! To begin, set your intention
to heal and then just trust your gut.

Sometimes the most productive thing to do is give yourself a rest
and indulge in the joy of missing out. I know it's difficult when you have
family, a job and responsibilities, but being a rebel can have its rewards.
Begin by setting a few new ground rules that can help you to preserve
your energy. This will enable you to recharge and rejuvenate. Make a
conscious effort to switch off from your computer, devices and screens
and take time off. Rest is essential for your wellbeing, and helps you
fast-track your gut healing.

OIL PULLING

An important practice to incorporate during the first four weeks and beyond is the healing art of oil pulling. Oil pulling is an ancient Ayurvedic ritual that has been credited with the rectification of many illnesses, including digestive troubles. The practice has an incredibly detoxifying effect, killing yeasts, bad bacteria, parasites, fungi and viruses in the mouth, including candida and streptococcus. By killing these microorganisms in the mouth, you'll prevent them from causing secondary infections in the gut, which can contribute to a range of illnesses throughout your body.

In Ayurvedic practices there are two oil-pulling techniques, kavala and gandusa. When you are practising kavala, you fill your mouth with liquid then close your mouth and hold the liquid there for a couple of minutes. After this, you begin to swirl the liquid around the mouth, then spit it out. The process shouldn't exceed more than three or four minutes and it is repeated two or three times. Gandusa is a different technique whereby you hold the liquid still in the mouth for three to five minutes and do not swish it around. You then spit the liquid out and repeat the process.

To oil pull with coconut oil, simply place 1 tablespoon (20 ml) extra virgin cold-pressed coconut oil in your mouth upon rising. It's best done on an empty stomach and before you've consumed any liquids. Swish the oil around your mouth for 10–20 minutes before spitting out.

Never swallow the oil, which will be full of bacteria. Brush your teeth thoroughly afterward, to remove any excess oil. It's best to buy a specific toothbrush for oil pulling, and wash it thoroughly using 3 percent hydrogen peroxide solution to prevent bad bacteria building up.

Including this simple ritual in your day will provide other benefits, including whiter teeth, clearer skin, healthier gums, fresher breath, clearer sinuses, for women better regulated menstrual cycles, an improved lymphatic system, better sleep and increased energy. It's a terrific, simple practice that will provide immense health benefits. It's well worth the swish!

EPSOM SALTS BATHS

Make time for yourself to have an Epsom salts bath at least twice a week. When you have a bath with Epsom salts, the magnesium sulfate is absorbed through the skin, and draws toxins from the body. It also sedates the nervous system to relax you completely, reduces swelling, loosens muscles, relieves muscular aches and pains, and is even a natural emollient and exfoliator.

MORE GREAT DETOX TECHNIQUES

If you have one available to you, try to visit a sauna or steam room to relax your muscles and promote sweating and detoxing through the skin. It's a therapeutic way to improve your circulation and create more effective blood flow through your body while cleansing. Heat has an analgesic, or pain relieving, effect on your body. It also helps you relax and unwind, and reduces tension in your muscles.

Saltwater flushes and enemas can also aid your body in detoxification.

NATURAL ANTIBIOTICS AND ANTIMICROBIALS

As discussed in Part One, a number of supplements can be used as natural antimicrobial options. They all have varying levels of antiviral, antifungal (and so anti-yeast) and anti-parasitic action. They include garlic, oil of oregano, black walnut, burdock root, goldenseal, olive leaf extract, grapefruit seed extract and pau d'arco. The table on pages 76–77 gives a breakdown of what each supplement does.

When healing myself I used natural garlic only, as I was staying away from supplements, but if you prefer you can use any of them to help the process. The most powerful ones are olive leaf extract and oil of oregano. They both taste extremely bitter and aren't very palatable, but if you're going to take them, follow your naturopath's directions and start with really small amounts.

It's important to remember with any antibiotic therapy to follow up with probiotics to repopulate the gut. If you don't want to use fresh garlic, then taking it in capsule form (odorless) is okay. Some people are susceptible to bloating and gas when consuming garlic, so your choice of natural antibiotic needs to be a personal one. I ate garlic raw every day and it really helped with my symptoms. It's extremely effective against yeast, fungal and viral infections.

During phase two of my healing I included a natural cleansing formula called diatomaceous earth. As many gut issues can be traced back to an unclean and inefficient digestive tract, I used diatomaceous

---

HOW TO MAKE AN EPSOM SALTS BATH

The best way to make an Epsom salts bath is to add 2 cups (17 fl oz/ 500 ml) Epsom salts to a warm bath while the water is running. Once the bath is at the right level and temperature for you, climb in slowly and let your body soak for 15–20 minutes.

earth to help clean out the accumulated build-up of waste, toxins, heavy metals and mucus in my digestive tract. It's also antibacterial, antiviral, antifungal and anti-parasitic. Food-grade diatomaceous earth can be purchased online.

Once my digestive system was cleaned, I noticed I had better digestion and waste removal, and increased nutrient absorption. As mentioned earlier, 70–80 percent of your immune system is located inside your digestive system, and a clean digestive tract helps the immune system work more efficiently. Importantly, the process of regularly and gently cleaning your pipes is a better option than constant dramatic colon purges and enemas.

Your digestive tract is like your teeth, in that plaque and waste continually build up there, so it's beneficial to "sweep away" these impurities on a daily basis and keep your colon toned, clean and efficient.

ANTIMICROBIAL SUPPLEMENTS AND THEIR EFFECTS

OIL OF OREGANO	Contains carvacrol and thymol, two powerful phenols that have the ability to kill harmful microbes in the body. It's a strong antioxidant with anti-inflammatory properties. It's also antibacterial, antiviral, antifungal and anti-parasitic. It's effective in killing staphylococcus bacteria. Good for short-term use. Very strong-tasting.
BURDOCK ROOT	Helps eliminate heavy metals from the body. The plant is antibacterial, antifungal and carminative (prevents gas). It has soothing, mucilaginous properties and can be taken as a supplement or a tea. Note that burdock has been associated with poisonings because some products have been contaminated with root of belladonna (deadly nightshade), which contains a poisonous chemical called atropine.
BLACK WALNUT	Contains astringent compounds that shrink inflamed tissues of the digestive system and help kill parasites. It can be effective in enhancing the elimination of various microbes from the bowel. It's also recognized by herbalists as a thyroid stimulant, since it's relatively rich in the trace mineral iodine. The tannins in black walnut encourage the elimination of unwanted microbes in the colon, as the acidic nature of tannins makes life uncomfortable for the alkaline-loving yeasts and microbes that can infect the bowel. It also contains bitter compounds that are antifungal and decrease the secretion of fluids in the digestive system.

SUPPLEMENTS THAT HEAL

Now that you've been detoxing your body and healing your gut, your body will have used alkaline minerals such as calcium, magnesium, sodium and potassium to process cellular debris and counter increased uric acid production. It's important to ensure that you're consuming adequate amounts of these minerals in your diet and that you're absorbing them too. If not, the body will remove calcium and magnesium from your bones and teeth to combat the lost minerals.

One of the most important vitamins to include when detoxing is vitamin C, which is a powerful antioxidant that helps the body break down toxins, allowing them to be flushed out of the body. A diet high in vitamin C-rich foods also works to stabilize free radicals, lowering the risk of chronic diseases.

GOLDENSEAL	Helpful in managing diarrhea and can assist with intestinal infections. A goldenseal tea can be used for three months to detoxify the body. It can also help support the immune system. Taking too much goldenseal for more than three months can lead to problems of the digestive tract, including constipation and diarrhea. It may also trigger extreme states of stress and, in some cases, delirium hallucinations.
OLIVE LEAF EXTRACT	The leaf of the olive tree contains an active phytochemical called oleuropein, which can help eliminate viruses and bacteria from within the digestive tract. Oleuropein foils viruses in a number of different ways, including: interfering with the amino acid production processes needed for viruses to replicate; penetrating infected cells and irreversibly inhibiting the ability of viruses to replicate; and neutralizing enzymes needed for replication and growth of viruses. Olive leaf extract contains flavonoids, which have been found to have strong anti-inflammatory benefits. It's also antiviral and effective against *Candida albicans*. It has a very overpowering taste.
GRAPEFRUIT SEED EXTRACT	Can be taken by mouth for bacterial, viral and fungal infections, including yeast infections. Grapefruit seed extract helps alkalize the body and stimulates the immune system. Again, it has a very overpowering taste and can irritate the digestive tract in some people.
PAU D'ARCO	Contains a chemical called lapachol, which gives the herb its strong immunity-boosting capability. It helps remove impurities, or toxins, from the body and balance bacteria in the gut. Tea is a good way to consume it.

As I was detoxing, I included a Supercharged Shake (see page 104) to help me with vitamin and mineral deficiencies on the days I felt exhausted and depleted. I created this fortifying shake because it not only delivers vitamins and minerals, but also recharges your immune system. I used non-synthetic powders and included calcium citrate, magnesium citrate, dairy-free probiotic powder (see opposite) and vitamin C. The best time to have this shake is at breakfast. Combining it with good fats, such as a tablespoon of coconut oil, will help your body absorb the nutrients faster. I wouldn't recommend having it every day, but it's good to consume three times a week when you're healing.

Along with the Supercharged Shake, I took krill oil about three times a week; it's a potent anti-inflammatory and I used it to help my arthritic symptoms and boost my immune system. When I was healing, however, I preferred to stick to food and keep my supplements at a very low level.

Many of the gut programs you'll see include endless lists of supplements that aren't always necessary, don't take the individual into account and are also expensive. By following my simple protocol and doing things naturally, you'll be taking things slowly and not overwhelming your body with synthetic supplements. If you do, however, decide to take supplements, it's good to ensure they're non-synthetic and contain no additives or sugars, and that you speak with your healthcare provider about dosages and timings.

Some of the optional vitamins and minerals that support gut and autoimmune health, which you could look into to relieve your individual symptoms, are:

* **VITAMIN A:** This plays a key role in supporting immune and inflammatory functions in the digestive tract, which is made up of mucosal tissues. These tissues secrete compounds that aid digestion. Vitamin A nourishes your mucosal tissues, helping to ensure that each organ in your digestive tract can function properly. It also aids the increased production of mucins to restore the mucosal layer of the gut lining.
* **B VITAMINS:** These are the most important vitamins for digestive health, as they help break down the nutrients in your food.
* **VITAMIN D:** Your digestive tract contains a large network of nerves that communicate to regulate your digestion. Vitamin D helps control the levels of calcium in your system so your nerve cells have access to the calcium they need to function.
* **VITAMIN E:** The body needs vitamin E to boost its immune system so it can fight off invading bacteria and viruses. Vitamin E also inhibits inflammation.

* **VITAMIN K2:** This is an important micronutrient normally produced by the healthy gut flora. People with disrupted gut flora could be deficient in K2.
* **L-GLUTAMINE:** This provides nutritional support for the gastrointestinal mucosa as well as supporting a healthy immune system.
* **ZINC:** This abundant trace element in the body is essential for growth and development, immune function, and gut health and healing.
* **POTASSIUM:** This element is essential for the heart, kidneys, muscles, nerves and digestive system to operate effectively.
* **COD LIVER OIL:** The vitamin A in cod liver oil helps build strong mucosal linings, particularly in the lining of your digestive tract.
* **FOLIC ACID:** Intestinal mucosal cells need a constant supply of folic acid (or folate), which is also necessary for iron absorption.

PROBIOTICS AND PREBIOTICS

Included in my Supercharged Shake is a high-potency, dairy-free probiotic powder to add beneficial flora back into the gut. It's important to do this once you've detoxed and cleansed your body, and have eliminated bacteria and yeasts from your gut. Probiotics are live microorganisms that are similar to the "good bacteria" found in a healthy human gut. Probiotics are available through foods or dietary supplements such as tablets and powders. Part of the problem with using cheap over-the-counter probiotics is that they consist of only a few strains, and are expensive. Look for brands that are non-synthetic and offer the full spectrum of probiotics, and speak to your naturopath about identifying which strains will be beneficial for you and your own particular condition and symptoms.

On page 88 you'll find a list of probiotic foods you can include in your diet to boost your good gut flora. In addition to probiotics, you may read about prebiotics being beneficial for gut healing. Prebiotics are indigestible carbohydrates that create balance in gut flora by promoting the growth and multiplication of beneficial probiotic microorganisms and preventing the growth of harmful bacteria. When you're looking for a probiotic, check if it has added fructo-oligosaccharides (FOS) and/or inulin. These are prebiotic substances touted as aiding the proliferation of good bacteria, but a lot of FOS is manufactured via chemical synthesis and can cause abdominal distress, especially in people with an overabundance of bad bacteria. For this reason, it's important to find the best probiotic that works for you and to look for natural prebiotics from your food. Flip over to page 88 to discover which foods are prebiotic.

NINE GUT-HEALING HERBALS

Here are nine symptom-soothing natural healers that have edged their way into mainstream medicine:

1 **ECHINACEA:** an effective antibacterial and blood-cleansing agent. Echinacea increases the level of a chemical called properdin that activates the part of the immune system responsible for strengthening defence mechanisms against viruses and bacteria.

2 **ANDROGRAPHIS:** an anti-inflammatory and antioxidant that stimulates one or more aspects of the immune reaction. It reduces fever; increases resistance to physical, emotional or biological stressors; and restores balance to the body.

3 **ASTRAGALUS:** an anti-inflammatory and antioxidant that stimulates one or more aspects of the immune reaction in time of chronic infection, debility or autoimmune disease. It increases resistance to physical, emotional or biological stressors; and restores balance to the body.

4 **LICORICE:** a root that increases the resistance to physical, emotional or biological stressors; restores balance to the body; reduces spasm of the respiratory tract; reduces the formation of mucus; and soothes inflamed mucous membranes of the respiratory tract.

5 **CINNAMON:** an antimicrobial that was found in a recent study to help suppress inflammation of the colon in mice, leading researchers to say that cinnamon extract may have significant anti-inflammatory effects in humans. It also reduces the sensation of nausea.

6 **YARROW:** an anti-inflammatory that promotes sweating during fever. Internally, yarrow acts as a soothing relaxant on the voluntary nervous system. It counteracts cramps and spasms of the stomach, abdomen and uterine system. At the same time, its bitter principles support the digestive system by acting on the gallbladder and liver.

7 **COMFREY:** a sealing and healing herb for the mucous lining of the digestive tract. It helps with irritation and inflammatory symptoms, and can be administered as an enema for absorption in the colon. The active components are allantoin and mucilage, which help renew healthy digestive cells.

8 **SLIPPERY ELM BARK:** a demulcent derived from the inner bark of the elm tree and used by traditional cultures. It soothes the lining of the digestive tract and creates a film over the mucous membranes, as well as absorbing toxins in the bowel and aiding faster elimination.

9 **ALOE VERA:** a gentle cleansing and healing herb that helps regularity and eases constipation and diarrhea.

A TYPICAL HEALING DAY, PHASE TWO

UPON RISING: Dry skin brushing followed by a hot shower. While you're in the shower, use extra virgin coconut oil to oil pull. There's a step-by-step guide for dry skin brushing on page 70 and for oil pulling on page 74.

EARLY MORNING: Enjoy a glass of hot water with lemon (see page 69) and add 1 teaspoon chopped raw garlic, or make your Supercharged Shake (see page 104).

BREAKFAST: Have a healing juice or smoothie like my Avocado Lassi (see page 112) or Berry Burst Smoothie (see page 111).

MID-MORNING: If you're taking an antimicrobial or supplements, take them now.

MORNING TEA: Drink a Curative Coffee (see page 136) and if you've finished the four-week elemental phase, snack on Lemony Herb Crackers (see my website) and dips. There's a bunch of delicious recipes that can take you from breakfast to midnight snacks on my website.

LUNCH: Enjoy some immune-boosting garlic soup.

AFTERNOON TEA: Savor an Overnight Edible Smoothie (see page 116).

DINNER: If you're still on the protocol, enjoy White Fish Soup with Saffron (see page 170), Celery, Leek and Thyme Soup (see page 169), Lemongrass Thai Soup (see page 178), or another soup made from sautéed, steamed or roasted vegetables combined with herbs, spices and Celtic or Himalayan sea salt. Blend with bone broth (see page 145), vegetable stock (see page 151) or filtered water. For a creamier soup, blend with coconut milk. If you're not on the protocol at this stage, enjoy an easily digestible meal, such as Shepherd's Pie with Cauliflower Mash or gluten-free Supercharged Lasagna (see my website for recipes).

NIGHT: Relax and soak in an Epsom salts bath (see page 75).

MAINTAIN AND RESTORE WITH FOOD

Once you've completed the four-week elemental diet and restored and rebalanced your gut bacteria with natural antibiotics and antimicrobials, your gut will have experienced a well-needed rest, and repaired and recovered from permeable holes and inflammation in your digestive tract. Your gut lining will now be able to provide a safe "home" for your gut bacteria to survive, thrive and fight against any bad guys that may make their way into your gut.

After working on your gut lining and starving and eliminating the bad bacteria, you'll now need to create and feed healthy communities of gut flora to boost your immune system, regulate hormones and improve brain function. There are many foods and supplements you can now begin to include to build this healthy community. Think of your gut as a garden that can only thrive when the soil is healthy. Healthy soil requires healthy foods and nutrients that will allow the "good guys" to flourish.

But first you need to make a small lifelong commitment to gut health and maintenance. Health cannot be attained through a quick-fix diet or a convenient pill; it requires you to make healthy choices every single day. After completing your four-week gut-healing protocol and cleanse and sweep, over the next four weeks (or when it feels right for you) you can do several things to ensure your gut health continues to improve.

EVERYDAY CHECKLIST

1. CUT OUT OR CUT DOWN ON GLUTEN
Based on everything we know about the effect of gluten on intestinal permeability (see page 18), it's safe to say it's something you should avoid if you want to continue to restore the health of your gut. Instead of consuming gluten-filled grains, stick to unrefined gluten-free grains such as buckwheat, quinoa and brown rice.

2. GO EASY ON THE SUGAR
Too much research points to the damage sugar is causing our health. Bad bacteria adore an abundance of sugar to feast on, and this includes overindulgence in fruit. Avoid all refined white sugar, as this is the worst kind. Stevia is a wonderful sugar-free alternative or, where you would use sugar in small amounts, opt for rice malt syrup, or try using fruit to bring out the sweetness in your food. When eating fruit,

eat a maximum of one piece a day, or choose to eat low-fructose options, such as berries, lemons, limes and grapefruit.

3. GO CRAZY WITH VEGETABLES

Your gut just loves easy-to-digest foods, and plant foods are gentle on the stomach. Eat an abundance of chlorophyll-rich greens, vegetable juices, and earthy vegetarian soups made from prebiotic-rich root vegetables, to ensure your good bacteria are nourished with lots of antioxidants, enzymes and nutrients for healthy digestion.

4. EAT FERMENTED FOODS DAILY

Once your gut lining is healed and only when you're ready, you can start to incorporate one cultured food such as Cultured Vegetables (see page 230), Easy-to-make Sauerkraut (see page 233), Kimchi (see page 232), Coconut Kefir (see page 124) or Homemade Kombucha (see page 236) to colonize your gut with healthy flora and boost your inner ecosystem. When starting out with fermented foods, only have a quarter of the recommended amount per serving or start with just 1 teaspoon and work your way up. Eating a range of different fermented foods will contribute a variety of bacterial strains, which will bring the diversity needed for a healthy microbiota. There are loads of blogs and websites dedicated to fermented foods where you can find great recipes, and Part Three includes some easy-peasy recipes in "Fermented foods for when your gut is strong" (see page 229).

5. DRINK LOTS OF PURE, FILTERED WATER

Water is vital to your gut health as it helps flush out toxins, but conventional tap water contains fluoride and chlorine, both of which are damaging to microflora. Choose to invest in a good water filter and drink at least eight glasses a day. Adding lemon juice or apple cider vinegar to your water will aid your digestion and break up mucus in the body, freeing up your lymphatic system and boosting your immune response.

6. WHEN IN DOUBT, REMEMBER WHOLE FOODS

Based on all that I've shared, it's clear that the way to achieve optimal health is to choose foods in their closest state to nature. The more nature is disrupted in your food, the less likely it is that your gut bacteria will know how to handle it. Eat things that are natural and unprocessed.

Go organic and chemical-free wherever possible. Eat grass-fed meat and animal products in an amount that would be naturally available if mass meat production didn't exist. Choose to nourish your body with an abundance of plant foods. Eating in this way will provide you with all the nutrients your digestive system needs to function at its best, delivering healing nutrients to all the systems of your body.

REINTRODUCING FOOD

By now you'll be feeling excited about seeing your symptoms decrease and you'll feel better and have more energy, clearer skin and a better digestion. But for some of you, it might be hard to think about reintroducing food.

For the initial phases of the protocol, you've had a nutritional blueprint to follow, knowing what to eat and when, how to get organized and what to do to navigate detoxing. But now it's time to reintroduce food, you might be starting to wonder what you should be eating or whether your symptoms will return the moment you go back to regular eating. I hear you.

The transition can be tricky, and it's very tempting to return to unhealthy habits as soon as you feel better. Of course, it's not convenient to stay on a liquid diet forever, but you can't dive straight back into your old ways of eating either. You should navigate the transition period of reintroducing food slowly and steadily, so that the improvements you've made on the program are durable and you can go on living the healthy, full life you're meant to live with a repaired and replenished gut.

The next few weeks are critical, because your gut is still vulnerable, and when you go back to normal eating you'll need to take things slowly and listen attentively to what your body is telling you. But first, it's important to define what "normal eating" is.

I'm unaware, of course, of what your eating patterns were like before you started reading this book, but I myself never realized how food affected my body until I got really sick. After I completed the elemental diet, I gained so much awareness about the effect of food on my body – both positive and negative – that it changed the way I looked at food and nutrition forever. I now limit gluten, sugar and dairy, and that's what works for me, but everyone is different.

I'm not advising that you eat exactly the way I do, but I encourage you to be curious and open to trying new foods, experimenting with new recipes and fresh habits, and seeing how your body feels.

Consuming healthy, gut-friendly food as a new way of eating doesn't have to be boring, bland, expensive or time-consuming. You don't need exceptional cooking skills, pricey equipment or a personal chef. Once you start playing around with a few recipes and get a bit more familiar with the ingredients, you'll find that healthy food can be fun and delicious! Eating natural wholefoods is the cornerstone of a healthy gut and a healthy body, but that doesn't mean you can never indulge.

In my life I follow the 80/20 rule. I choose healthy, gut-friendly food 80 percent of the time and I indulge in my favorite treats 20 percent of the time. Remember that you are what you do consistently, not what you do once in a while. Nowadays, my treats are mainly healthy ones, like my homemade chocolate and muffins – but I also love gelato!

When it comes to reintroducing food, if you're craving your grandmother's famous carrot cake or you've been invited to a dinner party and can't resist that slice of pizza, go ahead and have it! But remember to enjoy it. Savor every bite and enjoy it mindfully. And most importantly: Don't. Feel. Guilty. Guilt triggers stress reactions in your body that are worse for your gut than the gluten in the pizza or the sugar in the carrot cake! It's really okay to indulge in treats and enjoy them.

And after some time, when nourishing your body with wholesome foods has become a habit, you'll feel so amazing that you won't even want that slice of cake or pizza. But before you get to the stage where you can indulge in your favorite treats once in a while, you'll need to reintroduce food very slowly and pay close attention to your body's response.

This can be the perfect time to do an elimination diet. This basically means that you eliminate certain foods for a period of time, usually three or four weeks, then slowly reintroduce specific foods one by one and monitor your symptoms. There are many variants of the elimination diet, but they usually all advise removing gluten, dairy, soy, eggs and corn. Other common offending foods you might want to eliminate are pork, beans and lentils, coffee, nuts and seeds, and nightshade vegetables (tomatoes, potatoes, peppers, eggplants, chili peppers and goji berries).

At the end of the elimination period, pick one food you cut out – such as gluten, or dairy – only one, and eat it (but don't overindulge). Notice how you feel over the next 48 hours. If you have no reaction after two days, eat that same food again and look out for any reactions. From there, based on how you feel, you can decide if you want to reintroduce that food into your diet on a regular basis.

Then, pick another food and follow the same steps. Throughout the diet and the reintroduction process, you need to pay very close attention to how you're feeling and track any physical, mental or emotional symptoms. Keep a food journal and monitor your sleep, mood, energy levels, digestion and skin. Note, for example, if you suffer insomnia, fatigue, joint pain, skin breakouts or rashes, headaches, changes in your bowel movements, bloating, brain fog or sinus issues.

The whole process will take between five and eight weeks depending on how many foods you've eliminated, but at the end of the experiment you'll have learned much about how your body responds to different foods. It's a very empowering tool, to become your own health investigator and figure out what's right for your body.

If you don't want to do an elimination diet, the best way to reintroduce solid food after being on the elemental diet is to start with steamed vegetables and soft foods such as casseroles, slow-cooked dishes, and steamed fish or chicken served with brown rice, buckwheat or quinoa.

Include easy-to-digest foods so your gut can slowly readapt to digesting solid food. I recommend keeping two days a week where you eat only liquid food or partake in an intermittent fast. This is especially helpful during the first few weeks while you're settling into eating solid food again.

Reintroduce raw foods very slowly. They require more work for your digestive system to process, so give your body plenty of time to get used to digesting them again.

As you can see, I'm not giving you a strict diet to follow or a ten-page list of foods to avoid, because we're all different. You might thrive on dairy products while someone else might get terrible symptoms from a single glass of milk! I encourage you to be your own leader and find out for yourself what works for your body. It's a trial-and-error process, so be patient. But it's also very rewarding and empowering.

SUPERCHARGED TIP

Life's not about being perfect and dogmatic. This will only cause more harm than good because of the stress it will create. It's about listening to your body, being loving and gentle, and doing what feels right for you.

PREBIOTICS

Some say that the phrase "You are what you eat" should *actually* be 'You are what your *bacteria* eat'. Did you know that your good bacteria need certain foods to survive? As mentioned earlier, these foods are classified as prebiotics. They're the specific foods that feed *your* good bacteria. More precisely, these are foods containing non-digestible but fermentable oligosaccharides that change the structure and activity of your gut flora – with the prospect of promoting the health of their host (that being *you*!).

Instead of taking questionable prebiotic supplements, it's really important to eat a wide range of fiber-rich vegetables to provide your body with prebiotics. Garlic, for example, is a wonderful prebiotic food, as it's not only a killer of bad bacteria, but also contains dietary fructins, prebiotics that feed specific strains of bacteria that are important for your health.

Foods high in soluble fiber are broken down in the large intestine into a gelatinous, viscous by-product that produces acids and gases promoting the growth of good bacteria. Foods high in soluble fiber are wonderful prebiotics and include sweet potatoes, brussels sprouts, asparagus, turnips, mangoes, avocados, strawberries and apricots.

Resistant starches are starches that remain undigested until they get as far as the large intestine, where they undergo the same process as soluble and insoluble fibers. Foods containing resistant starch include potatoes, lentils, nuts and seeds. Remember to reintroduce these foods to your diet at a snail's pace and see how your belly reacts to them.

PROBIOTICS

Now that the elemental phase is over and you're ready to consume probiotic-rich foods, you'll be able to recolonize your gut with the good bacteria needed for thriving health. Apart from helping out the brain as well as the immune system, probiotics have been linked to the reversal and healing of countless illnesses, from nasal congestion to acne.

Once your gut lining is healed, eating fermented foods is one of the most important things you can do to improve your health. Fermentation increases the beneficial bacteria, enzymes and vitamins in food, and makes their nutrients more bioavailable. This is no new trend. Almost all traditional cultures have included fermented foods in their diet.

Fermented foods can either be bought or made at home, and include yogurt (made using goat's milk, sheep's milk, coconut milk or coconut water), sauerkraut, kimchi, milk kefir, water kefir, kombucha and beet kvass.

There are hundreds of resources and recipes online to help you source cultures and learn to make these foods at home. Try my simple Coconut Kefir (see page 124) or coconut Kefir Yogurt (see page 253) or go to the fermented foods section (see page 229) and make Cultured Vegetables, Sauerkraut, Kimchi or delicious Fermented Salsa.

Consuming fermented foods and beverages like these alongside other foods will also help your body digest everything more effectively. Combining both prebiotic-rich foods and probiotics in your daily diet will provide you with the best chance of creating a healthy community of gut flora. A warning, though, to go slow with introducing fermented foods into your diet, as not everyone can handle them. When I was healing my gut I would get terrible symptoms from fermented foods and still have to eat them in moderation now.

If you're not ready for fermented foods and natural probiotics, you can supplement with a probiotic capsule. Look for a dairy-free, non-synthetic powdered probiotic with a healthy number of different strains. Ask your naturopath or nutritionist to conduct a stool test so you can find out which strains you need to be taking for maximum benefit. The best time to take probiotics is in the evening before bed, so they can work through your digestive system as you sleep.

NUTRIENTS

Polyphenol-rich foods are excellent to include in your overall gut-healing plan, as they're broken down by your gut bacteria into metabolites that increase good bacteria and decrease bad bacteria. Polyphenol-rich foods include berries, flaxseed meal, plums, cherries, hazelnuts, raw cacao, red wine (in moderation and only organic and preservative-free) and green tea.

A TYPICAL HEALING DAY, PHASE THREE

UPON RISING: Start with dry skin brushing followed by a hot shower. While you're in the shower, use extra virgin coconut oil to oil pull.

EARLY MORNING: Enjoy a glass of hot water with lemon.

BREAKFAST: Munch on cranberry and walnut granola or a delicious breakfast bowl and Supercharged Shake (see page 104).

MORNING TEA: Enjoy a natural probiotic food with a Cleanse and Renew Smoothie (see page 104) or Coconut Kefir (see page 124).

LUNCH: Savor a Cauliflower Crust Pizza (see my website) and a side of Cultured Vegetables (see page 230).

AFTERNOON TEA: Sip on a Choc Mint Hot Chocolate (see page 136) or a Spiced Almond Chai (see page 139).

DINNER: Enjoy Buckwheat Pasta with Flaked Trout, slow-cooked lamb shanks (both on my website) and a side of Cultured Vegetables (see page 230).

BEFORE BED: Take two probiotic capsules. Count your blessings.

DETOX YOUR LIFE

Now you've cleansed your gut, it's time to start detoxing your emotions, your household and the things you put on your skin. Food alone will not promise a thriving colony of healthy bacteria in your gut. Stress and emotional factors can override even the most perfect diet.

Stress can be both acute and chronic. Chronic, long-term stress that lingers for weeks is incredibly damaging to gut health. Stress causes many reactions within the gut, including changes in gastric secretions, gut motility, mucosal permeability, visceral (i.e. organ) sensitivity and barrier function. Evidence also suggests that our gut bacteria respond in damaging ways to our negative emotions and stress. The hormones secreted during a stress response contribute to the overgrowth of bad bacteria.

What is it that causes you stress? Figuring out the cause is the key. Is it something you can control? What lifestyle changes or decisions can you make to remove stress from your life? If the answer is unclear, exercise such as calming yoga, walking and swimming may help you deal with these issues. When was the last time you got out into the sunshine and connected with nature? Sunlight and exposing your bare feet to the ground (also known as earthing) have a healing impact on hormones and the brain. A series of these lifestyle changes, including a wholefoods diet, may be all you need to take the edge off.

Toxic relationships and toxic friendships could be the thing preventing you from achieving a peaceful mind and a healthy gut. Choose to surround yourself with positive, kind people. By detoxing your relationships and enjoying mutual life-giving human connections, you'll experience more joy, which your gut bacteria will love you for.

Meditation is another wonderful practice that can help you master your mind and emotions. While it requires discipline, it has been shown to have remarkable effects on emotional health and stress. Cultivate an attitude of gratitude; find three things each morning to be grateful for and meditate on them.

Did you know that contributing to your community is another way to decrease stress and improve your emotional life? Being generous toward other people is a powerful way of bringing a healthy emotional perspective to our own lives. It also boosts social connectedness and has even been shown to increase life expectancy!

What is it that causes you stress? Figuring out the cause is the key. Is it something you can control? What lifestyle changes or decisions can you make to remove stress from your life?

If stress and negative thought patterns are a deeper problem for you, counselling and psychology may be needed, and that's okay! It's so important for the sake of your health to deal with any lingering emotional issues. Your gut and your emotions are a two-way street. They both have the potential to affect one another negatively, so addressing the state of your mental health, not just the food you eat, is incredibly important.

YOUR HEALTHY HOME

Minimizing your toxic load is vital to maintaining a healthy gut. Toxins and chemicals that are breathed in or absorbed through the skin have to be dealt with by your gut's immune system. Taking the load off the good guys will free them up to do all of the health-promoting duties on their to-do list. This means eliminating toxins and harmful chemicals wherever possible.

Chemicals in household cleaning products have been linked to a range of illnesses. For example triclosan, a common ingredient in antibacterial hand soap, has been linked to endocrine disruption and is a known carcinogen. Give away anything with an ingredients list you can't understand, and replace the toxic products with simple, homemade or chemical-free options.

Almost all your chemical-laden cleaning products can be replaced by three ingredients: baking soda, white vinegar and lemon juice. They will kill harmful bacteria and leave your house squeaky clean without any detrimental side effects.

Now you're making the change to a healthier lifestyle. Yoga – check. Daily green juice – check. Purchasing organic produce – check, check, check. But have you given much thought to the harmful toxins that are living rent-free in your furniture, upholstery or the mattress you nestle into every night?

These harmful toxins are known as volatile organic compounds (VOCs). VOCs are carbon-based chemicals that can evaporate or easily get into the air at room temperature. This is the odor you might smell when the carpets are professionally cleaned or there's new paint on the walls. Not all VOCs have such a strong odor, however; some have none at all but still cause the same level of harm to the body. Such harmful effects can be headaches, dizziness, nausea and eye/nose/throat irritation. Continual long-term exposure to these toxins can result in them accumulating in your body, thus potentially increasing the risk of liver and kidney damage.

Common VOCs such as formaldehyde, benzene, acetone and ethylene glycol can be found in air fresheners, paint, varnish, upholstery fabrics, vinyl, cosmetics and mothballs. Common floor coverings are most often primary contributors to indoor air contamination, as are all types of synthetic carpets, carpet underlay and upholstery with synthetic foams, foam rubber, latex or plastic. This is because they either have VOC constituents or these are present in the adhesives used to install them.

Furniture or carpets with a chemical finish, such as stain repellents and brominated flame-retardants, are also unhealthy. At all costs, avoid recarpeting your home or ripping out carpets while you're pregnant.

Furnishings in the bedroom also contain chemicals, such as flame-retardants and stain-repellents. These are present in most foam mattresses, synthetic curtains, upholstery or carpets. Even the clothes you keep in your wardrobe, when dry-cleaned, emit toxic chemicals!

Try not to keep too many electrical and electronic appliances in your bedroom at the same time, such as computers, TVs and hi-fi systems, as they are also treated with brominated flame-retardants.

Mold is a major indoor air polluter, and can occur at all times of the year in damp areas of a house or apartment, especially in south-facing parts of the home. Poorly maintained air-conditioning systems can also spread mold throughout a house.

HOW TO CREATE A HEALTHY HOME

* Choose furnishings wisely – natural finishes such as oils, waxes and polishes are better than polyurethane, varnishes, melamine or paint, all of which can emit VOCs.
* When repainting, choose low-VOC options or natural paints. Paint can be a major source of indoor air pollution, especially when it's freshly applied. Old paints manufactured more than forty-five years ago contain high lead levels, so make sure your paint isn't flaking or creating lead dust.
* Ensure your gas heaters are flued (and cleaned). An unflued gas heater can emit dangerous vapors.
* Minimize the impact of cleaning products by sticking to low-harm options such as vinegar instead of bleach. Cleaning a house regularly is the key to a healthy home.
* Regularly air your house by opening the windows and doors to flush out dirt and mold.
* Instead of using artificial air freshener, open your windows wide, whenever possible. If you can't keep windows open, use natural odor eaters. A bowl of baking soda effectively absorbs odors. Alternatively, use natural fragrances such as potpourri or lavender, or better yet, burn essential oils for enhanced beneficial effects.
* Vacuum with a HEPA filter machine to keep dust mites at bay.
* Use indoor plants as natural air filters to cleanse the air of VOCs and other pollutants.
* Keep a doormat at the front or back door to stop dirt and pollutants being tracked through the house, or make residents take off their shoes to leave the dirt at the door.
* Choose carpets made from organic natural fibers such as wool, cotton, rattan or jute. Not only do they look and feel nicer, they're also much safer for you and the environment.
* Choose curtains, carpets and upholstery containing little or no brominated flame-retardants or stain-repellents.
* When buying a PC or monitor, look for the TCO'95 Ecolabel, which limits the amount of brominated flame-retardant in the product.
* If you've just redecorated your home or moved into a newly decorated one, airing it for a short period before you live in it will dilute the chemicals during their most potent stage. High levels of VOCs will nonetheless outgas for months, and in many cases will continue to outgas for years.
* It's impossible to live in a bubble and protect yourself from every harmful chemical you come into contact with, so just phase them out at your own speed and as required to fit in with your lifestyle.

DETOX YOUR SKIN

The skin is an organ of digestion, and 60 percent of what you put onto it is absorbed directly into your bloodstream. When you think about it, nicotine patches are designed to be placed on the skin so nicotine can be absorbed into the body, so why wouldn't the ingredients you layer on your skin every day leach into your system too? This is frightening, considering the average woman places approximately 515 chemicals on her skin each day.

The beauty industry loves to promote the promise of eternal youth, skyscraper lashes and a sun-kissed glow, but many scary truths are hiding behind these promises of beauty and allure. Nowadays, more than 10,000 chemical ingredients are permitted for use in the production of personal-care products. Pick one of those moisturisers up off the shelf next time you're shopping, and read the ingredients list – you'll no longer be surprised that this is true. The danger is that many of these chemicals have been scientifically linked to a range of harmful diseases and bodily reactions.

Common skincare ingredients, including sodium lauryl sulfate, polyethylene glycol, parabens, isopropyl myristate and phthalates, have been linked to a horrendous number of illnesses, ranging from immune-system disorders and allergies to cancer and infertility. Your gut desperately needs a break from having to cope with these toxins.

Taking these facts on board, it's really important to read the ingredient lists of your products and do your research so that you and your family are safe from their harmful effects. Bath, beauty and skincare products should be made with pure, organic oils, fragrances, butters and pigments, and should contain absolutely no synthetic preservatives, toxins, artificial fragrances, colors or mineral oils. I have personally scrapped every possible toxin from my beauty regime, including my everyday lotions and potions.

Once you've restocked your makeup bag and bathroom cupboards with safe, organic products, you'll notice an improvement in your overall health, which, in turn, will improve the way you look, especially in the long term.

Never let yourself be fooled by the large claims of the cosmetics industry. There's no doubt that beauty comes primarily from within. It's a huge misconception to think that layering ingredients on the outside of our bodies will make us beautiful. If you heal your gut and feed your body with a range of colorful, antioxidant-rich, chemical-free foods and healthy fats, you'll have bought yourself a one-way ticket to a healthy, thriving colony of bacteria that will manifest in natural, glowing gorgeousness.

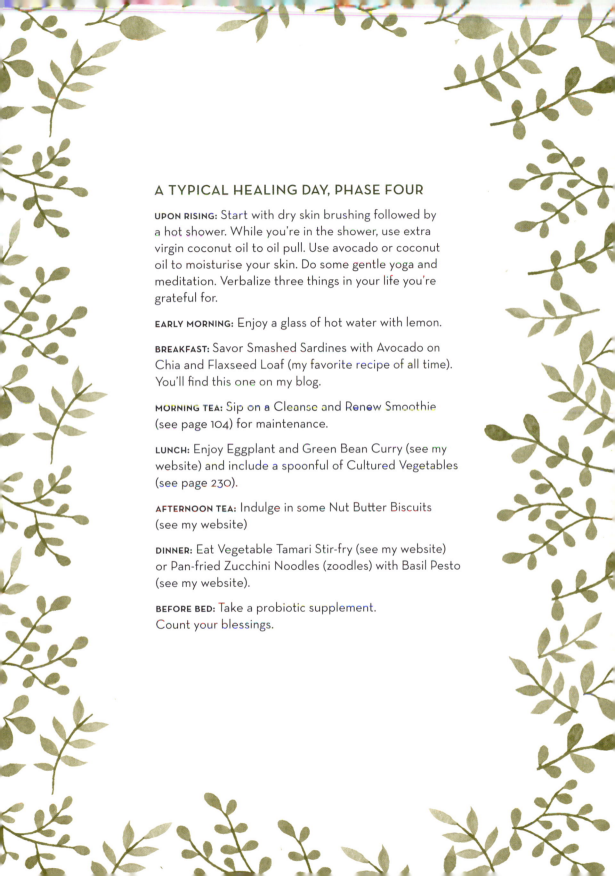

A TYPICAL HEALING DAY, PHASE FOUR

UPON RISING: Start with dry skin brushing followed by a hot shower. While you're in the shower, use extra virgin coconut oil to oil pull. Use avocado or coconut oil to moisturise your skin. Do some gentle yoga and meditation. Verbalize three things in your life you're grateful for.

EARLY MORNING: Enjoy a glass of hot water with lemon.

BREAKFAST: Savor Smashed Sardines with Avocado on Chia and Flaxseed Loaf (my favorite recipe of all time). You'll find this one on my blog.

MORNING TEA: Sip on a Cleanse and Renew Smoothie (see page 104) for maintenance.

LUNCH: Enjoy Eggplant and Green Bean Curry (see my website) and include a spoonful of Cultured Vegetables (see page 230).

AFTERNOON TEA: Indulge in some Nut Butter Biscuits (see my website)

DINNER: Eat Vegetable Tamari Stir-fry (see my website) or Pan-fried Zucchini Noodles (zoodles) with Basil Pesto (see my website).

BEFORE BED: Take a probiotic supplement. Count your blessings.

3

HEALING
RECIPES

Transform your tummy with
soothing, restorative and energy-
enhancing bowls of goodness.

A GUIDE TO THE ICONS

I've included little icons before each recipe so you can ensure
it meets your dietary needs. They will help you create a
personalized balanced and nourishing diet. See you later,
bloating and tummy trouble!

In some cases you'll need to choose the option for a
particular ingredient that suits your dietary needs – for
example, to make a vegetarian soup, choose the vegetable
stock rather than a meat broth.

Here's a breakdown of what each at-a-glance icon signifies.

▲ GF GLUTEN-FREE

Gluten is a mixture of proteins found in grains such as wheat,
rye, barley and oats. Some people can tolerate oats, but the
tricky bit is finding oats that haven't been contaminated by
wheat or other grains during processing. Symptoms of gluten
sensitivity can include gastrointestinal issues, skin problems,
changes in weight, headaches and depression. Gluten
sensitivity can make you feel ill or uncomfortable in your
gut, and can affect your mood and quality of life.

▲ WF WHEAT-FREE

Some people find wheat hard for their sensitive gut to digest
and that it can cause allergic reactions. Common symptoms of
a wheat allergy can include eczema, hives, asthma, hay fever,
IBS, tummy aches, bloated stomach, nausea, headaches, joint
pain, depression, mood swings and tiredness. Wheat products
can be replaced with buckwheat, rice, quinoa, tapioca and
wheat-free flours after the initial four-week period.

▲ DF DAIRY-FREE

To avoid dairy in the supermarket, look on labels for any food that contains cow's or goat's milk, cheese, buttermilk, cream, crème fraîche, milk powder, whey, casein, caseinate and margarines, all of which contain milk products. Substitutes for dairy milk can include nut and seed milks, and coconut milk. Butter and ghee are used in some recipes – see how you react to them.

▲ SF SUGAR-FREE

Sugar can contribute to nutrient deficiencies, as it provides energy without any nutrients. Researchers have reported that people with deficiencies of such vitamins, minerals and nutrients as magnesium, zinc, fatty acids and B-group vitamins are more likely to show symptoms of anxiety and depression.

▲ VEG VEGETARIAN

These recipes contain no meat, eggs or dairy products. To ensure you're eating enough of the essential nutrients needed for optimum health and gut healing, it's a good idea to include forms of protein, iron, B12, vitamin D and calcium in your diet. Good fats from non-meat sources are also very important. Eating a wide variety of real foods and not cutting out whole food groups unless absolutely necessary is a philosophy that works well for many people in the long term. Some recipes not marked VEG may still be suitable for lacto-ovo vegetarians – check the ingredients lists.

SHOPPING LIST

Here's your everyday shopping list for the four-week protocol and beyond.
 Remember to consume foods as close to their natural state as possible,
as it's much easier on the digestive system.

VEGETABLES
Arugula
Asian greens
Asparagus
Avocados
Beets
Bok choy
Broccoli
Brussels sprouts
Butternut squash
Cabbage
Carrots
Cauliflower
Celeriac
Celery
Cherry tomatoes
Chili peppers
Cucumbers
Daikon
Eggplants
English spinach
Fennel
French shallots
Garlic
Green beans
Kale
Lettuce
Mushrooms
Olives
Onions
Parsnips
Peas
Peppers
Rutabagas
Scallions
Snow peas
Sprouts (all types)
Swiss chard
Sweet potato
Tomatoes
Turnips
Watercress
Winter squash
Yellow button
 (pattypan) squash
Zucchini

EGGS
Eggs (organic, free-range)

DAIRY (FULL-FAT)
Butter (organic, unsalted)
Ghee

MEAT
Bacon/ham (sugar- and
 nitrate-free)
Beef and veal
Chicken
Duck
Lamb
Organ meats
Pork
Turkey

SEAFOOD
Anchovies
Fresh fish
Oysters
Salmon (wild-caught)
Sardines
Sashimi
Scallops
Sea vegetables
Shellfish
Shrimp
Squid
Tuna

FATS AND OILS
Butter (organic, unsalted)
Coconut oil (extra virgin)
Extra virgin olive oil
 (cold-pressed)
Ghee
Seed and nut oils (macadamia,
 walnut, sesame, flaxseed)

SEEDS, NUTS AND NUT BUTTERS
Almond butter
Almonds (slivered)
Brazil nut butter
Chia butter
Chia seeds
Flaxseeds (linseed)
Hazelnut butter
Macadamia butter
Nuts (activated)
Pecan butter
Pine nuts
Poppy seeds
Pumpkin seeds (pepitas)
Sesame seeds
Sprouted cereal
Sunflower seeds
Tahini
Walnut butter

GRAINS, FLOURS AND BAKING

Almond flour
Amaranth
Arrowroot flour
Arrowroot powder
Baking powder (gluten- and additive-free)
Baking soda
Brown rice
Brown rice crackers
Brown rice flour
Brown rice puffs
Buckwheat
Buckwheat flour
Buckwheat groats and pasta
Creamy buckwheat
Cacao butter
Cacao nibs
Cacao powder
Coconut butter
Coconut flakes
Coconut flour
Desiccated coconut
Golden flaxmeal
Granola (gluten-free)
Hazelnut flour
Millet
Quinoa
Quinoa flakes
Self-rising flour (gluten-free)
Tapioca flour
Vanilla beans
Vanilla essence (alcohol-free)
White rice

FRESH HERBS AND SPICES

Asafoetida
Basil
Cardamom
Chives
Cilantro
Cinnamon
Cumin (ground)
Cumin seeds
Curry leaf
Curry spices
Dill
Ginger
Mint
Nutmeg
Oregano
Parsley
Rosemary
Saffron
Sage
Thyme
Turmeric

CONDIMENTS AND SWEETENERS

Apple cider vinegar
Black pepper (fresh)
Celtic sea salt
Coconut aminos
Coconut milk
Coconut nectar
Dijon mustard
Dulse flakes
Nutritional yeast flakes
Stevia drops and/or powder
Tamari sauce (wheat-free)
Tomato paste
Vegetable stock (sugar- and additive-free)
Xylitol

MILKS AND DRINKS

Coconut water (from young coconuts)
Coffee (decaf)
Dandelion tea
Herbal teas/tisanes
Mineral/soda water
Nut milks
Tea (decaf)

FRUITS

Avocados
Berries (fresh and frozen)
Lemons
Limes

SUPPLEMENTS (OPTIONAL)

Calcium
Cod liver oil
Diatomaceous earth
Folic acid
Krill oil
L-Glutamine
Magnesium
Potassium
Probiotics
Slippery elm powder
Vitamins A, B, C, D and E
Zinc

Smoothies, juices and milks

Introducing smoothies and juices into your day will play a significant role in setting up firm foundations for lifelong health. My potent beverages will infuse vital nutrients, minerals and antioxidants into your gut at top speed, in an easy-to-digest and tasty way. Hello, fiber!

SUPERCHARGED SHAKE

▲GF ▲WF ▲DF ▲SF

SERVES 1

This shake contains all the essential vitamins and minerals for recharging your immune system. It will be your back-up to ensure you're not missing out on key immune-boosting nutrients, especially during the elemental phase (phase one).

1 cup (9 fl oz/250 ml) almond milk (see page 123)
1 organic egg (optional)
600 mg calcium citrate powder (follow instructions on packaging)
600 mg magnesium citrate powder (follow instructions on packaging)
1 teaspoon dairy-free probiotic powder (to be added in phase three)
1 teaspoon vitamin C powder with bioflavonoids

Pulse all the ingredients in a blender until smooth.

CLEANSE AND RENEW SMOOTHIE

▲GF ▲WF ▲DF ▲SF ▲VEG

SERVES 1

This highly detoxifying and tummy-soothing concoction will act as a spring-cleaning system for your digestive tract. Diatomaceous earth (DE) is an organic fossil shell flour that helps sweep out a build-up of plaque, acids, fungi and bad bacteria.

1 tablespoon diatomaceous earth (optional)
½ large ripe avocado, pitted and peeled
1 bunch (12½ oz/350 g) English spinach leaves
1 Lebanese (short) cucumber
2 stalks celery
1 cup (9 fl oz/250 ml) coconut water
½ cup (4 fl oz/125 ml) almond milk (see page 123)

Pulse all the ingredients in a blender until smooth.

Cleanse and Renew Smoothie

CUMIN DIGESTIVE AID (JEERA VELLAM)

▲ GF ▲ WF ▲ DF ▲ SF ▲ VEG

SERVES 4

Jeera is Hindi for "cumin" and *vellam* in this context means "water." Cumin is a powerful digestive aid and a detoxifier for the kidneys and bladder. Drink this shot after eating to improve digestion.

1 cup (9 fl oz/250 ml) filtered water
1 heaping teaspoon cumin seeds
1 inch (2.5 cm) piece of ginger, peeled and cut into thin sticks

Put all the ingredients in a small saucepan over medium heat and bring to a boil. Reduce the heat and simmer for 2 minutes.

Remove from the heat and set aside for 2 minutes before straining. Cool to room temperature and divide between four glasses to serve.

MORNING ELIXIR

▲GF ▲WF ▲DF ▲SF ▲VEG

SERVES 2

Enjoy this cleansing beverage first thing in the morning to kick-start your metabolism, detoxify your liver, alkalize your body and quash inflammation. It will give your gut a beautiful foundation for all the restorative recipes you'll be taking in each day.

> 2 tablespoons (40 ml) apple cider vinegar
> 2 tablespoons (40 ml) lemon juice
> 2 cloves garlic, crushed
> 2 inch (5 cm) piece of ginger, peeled and grated
> pinch of cayenne pepper (optional)
> 2 cups (17 fl oz/500 ml) filtered water
> liquid stevia or stevia powder, to taste

Put the apple cider vinegar, lemon juice, garlic, ginger and cayenne pepper in a teapot. Bring the filtered water to a boil, then add to the teapot and infuse for a few minutes.

Add stevia to taste, strain into two glasses and enjoy immediately.

NOTE: *This can also be made in bulk, strained into a glass bottle or jug and kept in the fridge. Drink it cold or reheat it in a saucepan over medium heat.*

Berry Burst Smoothie

BERRY BURST SMOOTHIE

▲ GF ▲ WF ▲ DF ▲ VEG

SERVES 2

This is such a delight to enjoy for breakfast or as an afternoon snack to power you through until dinner. Its bright-pink hue is aesthetically pleasing, and the smoothie itself provides your gut with powerful antioxidants that will target inflammation and free radicals.

1½ cups (13 fl oz/375 ml) almond milk (see page 123)
½ cup (4 fl oz/125 ml) additive-free coconut milk
½ cup (2½ oz/70 g) fresh or frozen mixed berries
1 tablespoon (16 g) nut butter (optional)
1 tablespoon (20 ml) lemon juice
¼ teaspoon liquid stevia or stevia powder

Pulse all the ingredients in a blender until smooth.

PURPLE POWER SMOOTHIE

▲ GF ▲ WF ▲ DF ▲ VEG

SERVES 2

Purple foods provide royal health benefits thanks to their rich concentration of healthy antioxidants and vital flavonoids such as anthocyanins. Their concentrations in these foods, say researchers, aid the positive modulation of gut bacterial populations.

1 Lebanese (short) cucumber
¼ small purple cabbage
½ cup (2¾ oz/80 g) frozen blueberries
½ cup (1 oz/25 g) English spinach leaves
1 tablespoon (16 g) nut butter
1½ cups (13 fl oz/375 ml) almond milk (see page 123)

Pulse all the ingredients in a blender until smooth.

AVOCADO LASSI

▲GF ▲WF ▲DF ▲SF ▲VEG

SERVES 1

Refreshing and cooling, this is a lovely blend to enjoy if you're suffering any noticeable gut discomfort. It will feel as light as a feather in your tummy and is deeply nourishing and filling.

1 small ripe avocado, pitted and peeled
1 cup (4¾ oz/135 g) ice cubes or crushed ice
¼ cup (2 fl oz/60 ml) coconut water
¼ cup (2 fl oz/60 ml) additive-free coconut milk, plus extra if required
liquid stevia or stevia powder, to taste

Put all the ingredients in a blender. Pulse to break up the ice, then blend until smooth. If the mixture is too thick, add a little more coconut milk.

ZESTED GINGER BEER

▲GF ▲WF ▲DF ▲SF ▲VEG

SERVES 1

Why reach for a can of fizzy drink overflowing with refined sugar and artificial colors when simple and delicious drinks like this one will energize your system? The ginger in this sparkling elixir will beat gut inflammation and soothe nausea.

1 teaspoon grated ginger
1½ tablespoons (30 ml) each of freshly squeezed lime and lemon juice
10 drops liquid stevia
1 cup (9 fl oz/250 ml) sparkling mineral water
1 teaspoon grated lime zest
ice and lime slices, to serve

Put the ginger, juice, stevia, mineral water and zest in a glass jar with an airtight screw-top lid. Screw the lid on tightly then shake gently.

Pour over ice and garnish with lime slices.

NOTE: *You can strain the ginger beer to remove the ginger pieces before drinking if you prefer.*

OVERNIGHT EDIBLE SMOOTHIE

▲GF ▲WF ▲DF ▲VEG

SERVES 1

Just as you may prepare a Bircher muesli overnight, this smoothie benefits from the same early preparation, leaving you with a deeper complexity of flavors, as they mingle while you're sleeping. If you lead a busy lifestyle, this is such a wonderful way to ensure a power-packed breakfast every morning.

½ cup (4 fl oz/125 ml) almond milk (see page 123)
½ cup (4 fl oz/125 ml) additive-free coconut milk
½ cup (2½ oz/70 g) frozen mixed berries
1 tablespoon (20 ml) lime juice
1 tablespoon (16 g) almond butter
1 teaspoon alcohol-free vanilla extract
grated zest of 1 small lime
pinch of stevia powder (optional)

Combine all the ingredients in a glass jar or bowl and refrigerate overnight.

In the morning, pour into a blender and blend until smooth.

NOTE: *If you don't have almond butter, substitute 1 tablespoon (5 g) raw almonds, remembering to blend well.*

Electrolyte Balancer

ELECTROLYTE BALANCER

▲GF ▲WF ▲DF ▲SF ▲VEG

SERVES 1

Enjoy this electrolyte-balancing drink twice a day (preferably upon rising and/or before meals) to help keep your body functioning well and stay hydrated.

> juice of ½ lemon
> 1 cup (9 fl oz/250 ml) warm filtered water
> 1 teaspoon Celtic sea salt

Combine all the ingredients and stir to dissolve the salt.

LEE'S GREEN JUICE

▲GF ▲WF ▲DF ▲SF ▲VEG

SERVES 1

My green juice has all the greens your body is shouting out for in an easy-to-prepare and well-balanced hit. This is a wonderful way to increase your energy first thing in the morning, thanks to its richness in circulation-boosting and blood-oxygenating chlorophyll.

> 1 bunch (12 oz/350 g) spinach
> 1 handful of mint
> 1 handful of flat-leaf (Italian) parsley
> 1 tablespoon (20 ml) lemon juice
> 1 Lebanese (short) cucumber, halved lengthwise
> a few lettuce leaves
> 4 stalks celery
> ¾–1¼ inch (2–3 cm) piece of ginger, peeled
> 6 ice cubes

With the motor running, feed all the ingredients except the ice cubes into a juicer one at a time.

Pour into a glass over the ice cubes and sip slowly to enjoy the juice's myriad benefits.

CASHEW MILK

▲GF ▲WF ▲DF ▲SF ▲VEG

MAKES 2¼ CUPS (19¼ FL OZ/560 ML)

Cashews are a wonderfully creamy dairy alternative and provide a good serving of minerals including copper, phosphorus, manganese, magnesium and zinc. Use cashew milk instead of dairy in teas, smoothies, mashes and soups. To pre-soak nuts, leave them in a bowl of filtered water for 2–3 hours.

3 cups (26 fl oz/750 ml) filtered water, boiled then cooled slightly
1 cup (5½ oz/155 g) natural cashews, pre-soaked
   (see above) and drained
¼ teaspoon alcohol-free vanilla extract
liquid stevia or stevia powder, to taste

Process the water, cashews and vanilla in a blender until smooth. Strain through a fine sieve, reserving the cashew pulp to use again (see below). Sweeten the cashew milk with stevia to taste, then pour into an airtight sterilised container and keep refrigerated for 4–5 days.

NOTE: *You can make more cashew milk (opposite right) by adding the cashew pulp to the blender with more water (this can be done up to three times). The cashew pulp will keep in a sealed container in the fridge for up to 3 days.*

L–R: Egg Milk (page 122); Cashew Milk

EGG MILK

▲GF ▲WF ▲DF ▲SF

MAKES 4 CUPS (35 FL OZ/1 L)

This vitamin- and mineral-rich drink (pictured on page 121) will really fast-track gut healing. For a deliciously warming chai version add ¼ teaspoon ground cinnamon, ¼ teaspoon ground nutmeg and ⅓ teaspoon ground cardamom.

3 organic eggs
4 cups (25 fl oz/1 L) warm or cold filtered water
¼ teaspoon alcohol-free vanilla extract
4 drops stevia (optional), or to taste

Beat the eggs in a blender at low speed, gradually adding the water. Add the vanilla and stevia, then pour into an airtight sterilized container and keep refrigerated for up to 3 days.

ALMOND MILK

▲GF ▲WF ▲DF ▲SF ▲VEG

MAKES 2¼ CUPS (19¼ FL OZ/560 ML)

Several varieties of almond milk can be found lining the shelves of your local supermarket. Unfortunately, many of these contain additives and yeast-feeding sugars. Making this recipe at home will ensure fresh-tasting milk that won't destroy your friendly gut flora.

3 cups (26 fl oz/750 ml) filtered water, boiled then cooled slightly
1 cup (5¾ oz/160 g) blanched almonds, pre-soaked (see page 120)
  and drained
¼ teaspoon alcohol-free vanilla extract
liquid stevia or stevia powder, to taste

Pulse the water, almonds and vanilla in a blender until smooth. Strain through a fine sieve, reserving the almond pulp to use again (see below). Sweeten the almond milk with stevia to taste, then pour into an airtight sterilized container and keep refrigerated for 4-5 days.

NOTE: *You can make more almond milk by adding the almond pulp to the blender with more water (this can be done up to three times). The almond pulp will keep in a sealed container in the fridge for up to 3 days.*

COCONUT KEFIR

▲GF ▲WF ▲DF ▲SF ▲VEG

SERVES 2

This cultured drink is laden with microbes that will help to restore your inner ecology after the elemental phase (phase one). With a wonderfully tart taste and lightly fizzy texture, this is the perfect tonic to be served cold and sipped throughout the day.

You'll need a sterilized glass jar, a blender, a strainer, a square of cheesecloth, an elastic band and a wooden spoon. Avoid using metal implements and store in glass.

1½ cups (13 fl oz/375 ml) coconut water or 1 young coconut,
   at room temperature
2 dairy-free probiotic capsules or 1 teaspoon dairy-free
   probiotic powder
liquid stevia or stevia powder, to taste (optional)

If using a young coconut, open and strain the water into the sterilized glass jar; if not, pour the coconut water straight into the glass jar. Add the contents of the probiotic capsules, or the probiotic powder, and stir with a wooden spoon. Cover the jar with the cheesecloth and secure with the elastic band, then place in a cool, dry, dark place for 1–2 days. It will be ready when the liquid turns from clear to cloudy white and there's no remaining sweetness.

Once it is ready, add stevia to taste, if using, and transfer to the fridge, where it will keep for up to 2 weeks.

Coffees, teas, toddies and tisanes

Be infused and enthused with my delicious
concoctions of coffees, teas, toddies and tisanes.
If you're hankering for a herbal, you'll love the
sweet simplicity of my Chamomile and Lavender
Tea, or the comforting effects of Soothing Sage,
Mint and Ginger Tea. Sleep tight with a Nutmeg,
Saffron and Cashew Nightcap or enjoy the
benefits of a Curative Coffee.

ANTI-INFLAMMATORY TODDY

▲ GF ▲ WF ▲ DF ▲ SF ▲ VEG

SERVES 1

Inflammation lies at the root of many chronic illnesses, and a majority of them start within the gut as an autoimmune reaction that develops into systemic inflammation. This tea is your drug-free weapon of prevention, laced with creamy cashew milk and perfumed with healing spices.

> 1 cup (9 fl oz/250 ml) cashew milk (see page 120)
> ½ teaspoon ground turmeric
> ¼ teaspoon ground cardamom
> ¼ teaspoon ground cinnamon
> ¼ teaspoon freshly grated ginger
> pinch of vanilla powder
> pinch of freshly cracked black pepper
> 6 drops liquid stevia

Heat the cashew milk in a small saucepan over medium heat for 2–3 minutes or until just warmed. Add the spices, ginger, vanilla and pepper, then stir to remove any lumps.

Remove from the heat and pour through a fine sieve to remove the grated ginger. Add the stevia and enjoy warm.

SUPERCHARGED TIP

Piperine, a key ingredient in black pepper, enhances the bioavailability of turmeric.

AROMATIC CURRY LEAF TISANE

▲GF ▲WF ▲DF ▲SF ▲VEG

SERVES 1

Curry leaf tea is a South Indian natural remedy used for centuries to cleanse and treat the digestive system. The smell and taste of fresh curry leaves stimulate salivary secretions, which in turn set off the secretion of digestive juices. To control indigestion and flatulence, add the ginger and a spoonful of dried and ground curry leaves.

Curry leaves can be purchased from your local Asian grocery store.

12 curry leaves, crushed with your hands to release the oil
1 teaspoon grated ginger (optional)
1 cup (9 fl oz/250 ml) warm filtered water
juice of ½ lime
liquid stevia or stevia powder, to taste

Put the curry leaves and ginger, if using, in a teapot, pour over the water then add the lime juice and stevia. Infuse for 5–10 minutes, then strain and drink immediately.

SUPERCHARGED TIP

Nurture a small potted curry leaf plant in your house. Curry plants are easy to maintain, as all they require is regular watering and protection from frosts if you have them. Besides a bunch of medicinal benefits, the curry leaf plant has the added advantage of repelling insects and ensuring a fresh aroma in the house.

NUTMEG, SAFFRON AND CASHEW NIGHTCAP

▲GF ▲WF ▲DF ▲SF ▲VEG

SERVES 1

This spicy nightcap will warm up your insides and flood your digestive system with anti-inflammatory medicinal spices. This is also a great one to serve when entertaining friends.

The first step is to prepare a masala powder, which you can then keep in a sealed container and use each time you make this tea.

MASALA POWDER

⅓ cup (2¾ oz/80 g) natural cashews
¼ cup (1½ oz/40 g) natural almonds
¼ cup (1¼ oz/35 g) unsalted pistachios, shelled
⅛ teaspoon saffron threads
6 cardamom pods, seeds only, pods discarded
¼ teaspoon ground nutmeg

NIGHTCAP DRINK

1 cup (9 fl oz/250 ml) cashew milk (see page 120)
1 tablespoon (7 g) masala powder, or to taste

To prepare the masala, pulse all the ingredients in a food processor until finely ground. Don't over-process or it will become a paste.

To make the nightcap, put the cashew milk in a small saucepan over medium heat. Add the masala and heat until warm. Don't let it boil.

Pour into a favorite drinking vessel and relax.

SUPERCHARGED TIP

....

Saffron is one of the most expensive spices. If it's beyond your budget, use ground cumin instead.

....

Chamomile and Lavender Tea

TURMERIC TEA

▲ GF ▲ WF ▲ DF ▲ SF ▲ VEG

SERVES 1

Turmeric is one of the most thoroughly researched plants in existence, with more than 5600 peer-reviewed biomedical studies indicating its preventative and therapeutic applications, particularly the role of its wonder ingredient curcumin in decreasing inflammation. This gorgeously golden tea is a wonderful way to savor its medicinal benefits.

    1 cup (9 fl oz/250 ml) almond milk (see page 123)
    2 teaspoons ground turmeric
    1 teaspoon grated ginger
    6 drops liquid stevia

Heat the almond milk in a small saucepan until it reaches room temperature. Put the turmeric and ginger in a mug. Pour a small amount of the warm milk over the spices in the mug and stir to create a liquid paste, ensuring there are no lumps. Add the remaining milk, stirring well, and sweeten with the stevia.

CHAMOMILE AND LAVENDER TEA

▲ GF ▲ WF ▲ DF ▲ SF ▲ VEG

SERVES 2

The combination of these two delicate and calming herbs will settle your nervous system and relax your digestive system, especially if you're feeling stressed or tense.

    2 teaspoons lavender buds
    2 teaspoons chamomile buds
    2 cups (17 fl oz/500 ml) boiling filtered water
    1 tablespoon (20 ml) lemon juice

Put the lavender and chamomile in a teapot. Pour over the water, then add the lemon juice. Infuse for 10 minutes, then pour into mugs or glasses (or strain it if you prefer) and serve.

CHOC MINT HOT CHOCOLATE

▲ GF ▲ WF ▲ DF ▲ SF ▲ VEG

SERVES 1

Don't drink this too late at night, as the cacao may give you a buzz and keep you awake. It's best drunk in the morning and as an occasional treat.

   2 teaspoons raw cacao powder
   ¼ teaspoon ground cinnamon
   ¼ teaspoon alcohol-free peppermint essence
   ½ cup (4 fl oz/125 ml) almond milk (see page 123)
   ½ cup (4 fl oz/125 ml) additive-free coconut milk
   7 drops liquid stevia or ⅛ teaspoon stevia powder

Put the cacao powder, cinnamon and peppermint essence in a small heavy-based saucepan. Add 2 tablespoons of the almond milk and stir over medium heat until thoroughly mixed. Add the remaining almond milk and the coconut milk, then stir frequently until warmed through. Stir through the stevia and drink immediately.

CURATIVE COFFEE

▲ GF ▲ WF ▲ SF

SERVES 1

Bulletproof your digestive system with the healing powers of coconut oil. This coffee (pictured on page 142) is so thick, rich and creamy, you won't even notice you've given up your regular caffeine fix.

   1 cup (9 fl oz/250 ml) Swiss-water-processed decaf coffee made
      with hot filtered water, then cooled slightly
   2 teaspoons unsalted raw butter (omit if lactose-intolerant)
   2 tablespoons (40 ml) extra virgin coconut oil

Pulse all the ingredients in a blender for 30 seconds or until well combined and frothy. Pour into a mug and sip slowly.

Choc Mint Hot Chocolate

SPICED ALMOND CHAI

▲GF ▲WF ▲DF ▲SF ▲VEG

SERVES 4

Traditional chai is known within Ayurvedic medicine to have myriad health-promoting properties. Drinking chai regularly will increase what Ayurveda refers to as digestive fire and we would call metabolism. This means it will soothe and relax the digestive tract, increase the release of toxins and curb a raging appetite.

4 cups (35 fl oz/1 L) almond milk (see page 123)
½ teaspoon alcohol-free vanilla extract
¼ teaspoon ground cinnamon, plus extra to serve
¼ teaspoon ground nutmeg
¼ teaspoon garam masala
¼ teaspoon stevia powder

Mix the almond milk, vanilla, cinnamon, nutmeg and garam masala in a heavy-based saucepan over medium heat until just simmering. Remove from the heat, stir in the stevia, pour into mugs and top each with a pinch of cinnamon.

SOOTHING SAGE, MINT AND GINGER TEA

▲ GF   ▲ WF   ▲ DF   ▲ SF   ▲ VEG

SERVES 2

This warming mixture is the ultimate tummy-soother. Refreshing sage and mint leaves combined with the anti-inflammatory, anti-emetic and appetite-reducing effects of ginger make this brew perfect during phase one of the gut-healing protocol.

> 1 inch (2.5 cm) piece of ginger, peeled and sliced
> 1 handful of mint leaves
> 1 tablespoon (2 g) roughly chopped sage leaves
> 2½ cups (21½ fl oz/625 ml) boiling filtered water
> squeeze of lemon juice
> liquid stevia or stevia powder, to taste

Put the ginger in a warmed teapot or jug and add the mint and sage leaves. Add the water and lemon juice, cover the lidded teapot or the jug with a tea towel and infuse for 15 minutes.

Pour into a mug (straining it, if you like), add stevia to taste and serve.

SUPERCHARGED TIP

Traditionally, sage is used to treat a weakened nervous and digestive system.

Curative Coffee (left/page 136); Dandy Chai Latte (right)

DANDY CHAI LATTE

▲GF ▲WF ▲DF ▲SF ▲VEG

SERVES 2

There's no need to miss out on steamy sweet drinks while healing your gut. This dandy darling is a tummy-friendly take on the conventional refined-sugar and dairy variety. Dandelion is also a brilliant anti-inflammatory, gut-detoxifying replacement for black tea or coffee.

3 cardamom pods
1 star anise
4 cloves
2 cups (17 fl oz/500 ml) almond milk (see page 123)
5 drops liquid stevia
2 lactose-free dandelion tea bags
2 inch (5 cm) piece of ginger, peeled and thinly sliced
1 cinnamon stick
pinch of grated nutmeg, to serve (optional)

Lightly crush the cardamom pods, star anise and cloves with the back of a spoon. Put in a small saucepan and add the almond milk and stevia. Place over medium heat and bring to a boil, then reduce the heat to low and simmer for 5 minutes.

Remove from the heat, add the tea bags, ginger and cinnamon, and stir gently. Cover the pan and infuse for 3 minutes.

Strain, then allow to cool slightly. Serve as is or sprinkled with nutmeg.

NOTE: *If you have a hand-held milk frother, now's the time to get frothing.*

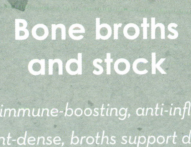

Bone broths and stock

Soothing, immune-boosting, anti-inflammatory and nutrient-dense, broths support digestion by healing and sealing the digestive tract. They contain gelatin, which attracts and holds liquids to fully support digestion, and boast a rich array of easily absorbable minerals such as calcium, magnesium, phosphorus, silicon, sulfur and trace minerals. They even contain material that's beneficial for arthritis and joint pain.

CHICKEN BROTH

▲ GF   ▲ WF   ▲ DF   ▲ SF

MAKES ABOUT 4 CUPS (35 FL OZ/1 L)

Your grandfolks were right in prescribing chicken soup when you were feeling under the weather. Not the styrofoam-cup variety, of course. Real chicken broth has natural properties that repair and calm the mucous lining of the small intestine, improving digestion and soothing the nervous system.

> 1 whole organic chicken
> 2 chicken feet for extra gelatin (optional)
> 8 cups (68 fl oz/2 L) filtered water
> 2 tablespoons (40 ml) apple cider vinegar
> 2 tablespoons (40 ml) lemon juice
> 1 large onion, chopped
> 3 stalks celery, chopped
> Celtic sea salt and pepper, to taste
> 1 bunch (3½ oz/100 g) flat-leaf (Italian) parsley
> 2 cloves garlic, crushed

Put the chicken and chicken feet in a large stainless-steel stockpot with the water, apple cider vinegar, lemon juice, onion, celery, and salt and pepper. Bring to a boil over medium heat, skimming off any foam that rises to the top. Reduce the heat to the lowest setting, then cover and simmer for 2 hours.

Remove from the heat, remove the chicken from the pot and take the meat off the bones, reserving the bones and setting aside the meat for another use.

Return the bones to the pot and simmer over very low heat for 4–6 hours, checking from time to time and adding a little more filtered water if necessary. Ten minutes before removing from the heat, add the parsley and garlic.

Remove the bones with a slotted spoon, strain the broth into a large bowl, and refrigerate until the fat congeals on top. Skim off the fat and store the broth in an airtight container in the fridge or freezer, or freeze in ice-cube trays.

SUPERCHARGED TIP

....

Cooked chicken can be frozen for later use. Break it up, spread it on parchment paper and freeze in layers in a freezer-proof container.

....

BEEF BROTH

▲GF ▲WF ▲DF ▲SF

MAKES 4 CUPS (35 FL OZ/1 L)

Beef bones produce a mineral-rich wobbly broth, thanks to their abundance of gelatin. While you're on the elemental diet of phase one, this broth will act as a "protein sparer," helping you make the most of any proteins you consume. Marrow or knucklebones work well for this broth.

¼ cup (2 fl oz/60 ml) extra virgin coconut oil
2 lb 4 oz (1 kg) beef bones
8 cups (68 fl oz/2 L) filtered water
2 carrots, peeled and roughly chopped
2 stalks celery, roughly chopped
3 cloves garlic
1 onion, peeled and quartered
1 bay leaf
2 tablespoons (40 ml) apple cider vinegar
Celtic sea salt and freshly cracked black pepper, to taste

Preheat the oven to 400°F/gas mark 6 (200°C).

Place a flameproof casserole dish on the stovetop over medium heat and melt the coconut oil. Add the bones and stir to coat. Add the lid and transfer the casserole dish to the oven. Bake for 30 minutes or until the bones are browned.

Transfer to the stovetop, cover with the filtered water and add the remaining ingredients, including the seasoning. Bring to a simmer, then reduce the heat to as low as possible and simmer for 4–6 hours, checking from time to time and adding a little more filtered water if necessary.

Remove from the heat, allow to cool, then strain and refrigerate until the fat congeals on top. Skim off the fat and store the broth in an airtight container in the fridge or freezer, or freeze in ice-cube trays.

SUPERCHARGED TIP

Apple cider vinegar helps draw valuable minerals from the bones, to supercharge your broth and fast-track gut healing.

LAMB BROTH

▲GF ▲WF ▲DF ▲SF

MAKES ABOUT 4 CUPS (35 FL OZ/1 L)

Think before you throw out the trimmings and bones from your next lamb roast. Lamb broth provides similar nutritional benefits to a gelatin-rich beef broth, but with the comforting flavor of lamb to add variety to your soups.

¼ cup (2 fl oz/60 ml) extra virgin coconut oil
2 lb 4 oz (1 kg) lamb marrow bones
8 cups (68 fl oz/2 L) filtered water
2 carrots, peeled and roughly chopped
2 stalks celery, roughly chopped
3 cloves garlic
1 onion, peeled and quartered
1 bay leaf
2 tablespoons (40 ml) apple cider vinegar
Celtic sea salt and freshly cracked black pepper, to taste

Preheat the oven to 400°F/gas mark 6 (200°C).

Place a flameproof casserole dish on the stovetop over medium heat and melt the coconut oil. Add the bones and stir to coat. Add the lid and transfer the casserole dish to the oven. Bake for 30 minutes or until the bones are browned.

Transfer to the stovetop, cover with the filtered water and add the remaining ingredients, including the seasoning. Bring to a boil, then reduce the heat to as low as possible and simmer for 4–6 hours. Add a little more filtered water from time to time if necessary.

Remove from the heat and allow to cool, then strain and refrigerate until the fat congeals on top. Skim off the fat and store the broth in an airtight container in the fridge or freezer, or freeze in ice-cube trays.

SUPERCHARGED TIP

Make bone broths in a slow-cooker – cook on low for up to 24 hours, topping up with filtered water if the liquid reduces too much.

VEGETABLE STOCK

▲GF ▲WF ▲DF ▲SF ▲VEG

MAKES 4–5 CUPS (35–44 FL OZ/1–1.25 L)

A stock with a savory flavor punch is the key foundation for scrumptious soups, especially delicate summer soups. Proportions don't need to be to the lettuce, oops, letter – just throw in what you have and create a melting pot of goodness. Use top-quality vegetables and be bold with healing seasonings.

2 large onions, skin on, quartered or thickly sliced
2 parsnips, rinsed and roughly chopped
2 stalks celery, roughly chopped
1 leek, roughly chopped
3 cloves garlic, skin on
1 red pepper, quartered and seeded
2 roma (plum) tomatoes, halved
extra virgin olive oil, for drizzling
1 small bunch (2 oz/55 g) flat-leaf (Italian) parsley
4–5 thyme sprigs
2 bay leaves
1 teaspoon whole black peppercorns
⅓ cup (2½ fl oz/80 ml) apple cider vinegar
filtered water, to cover

Preheat the oven to 400°F/gas mark 6 (200°C).

Put all the vegetables in a roasting pan and splash with the olive oil, tossing to coat.

Roast for 45 minutes, stirring often. You may have to remove the vegetables that cook faster as they are ready. Once all the vegetables are cooked, transfer them to a large stockpot or flameproof casserole dish over medium heat on the stovetop. Add the herbs, peppercorns and apple cider vinegar, then add filtered water to cover and bring to a boil. Reduce the heat to low and simmer for 1 hour.

Strain through a cheesecloth-lined sieve, store in an airtight container in the fridge and use as needed.

Healing and sealing soups

While healing your gut, one of the most nourishing and easy foods you can include in your weekly meal plan is soup. Not only is it a one-pot wonder, but you can store it easily in your fridge or freezer to grab on those days you don't feel like cooking.

PEA, SPINACH AND LAMB SOUP

▲GF ▲WF ▲DF ▲SF

SERVES 4

Imagine the most scrumptiously robust Sunday roast blended into a satisfying soup! This recipe is an easily digestible version of a triumphant and meaty meal, with the valuable benefits of bone broth to repair and heal your gut lining.

1 bulb garlic, whole, unpeeled
extra virgin olive oil for roasting, plus extra to serve
2 tablespoons (40 ml) extra virgin coconut oil or 1 tablespoon (20 ml) ghee
1 onion, diced
3 sprigs thyme, leaves picked
10½ oz (300 g) lamb fillets or backstrap, thinly sliced
4 cups (35 fl oz/1 L) beef broth (see page 147)
3⅓ cups (1 lb 2 oz/500 g) freshly shelled or frozen peas
1 cup (1½ oz/45 g) baby spinach leaves
1 tablespoon (20 ml) apple cider vinegar
1 handful of flat-leaf (Italian) parsley, roughly chopped, or micro parsley
Celtic sea salt and freshly cracked black pepper, to taste

Preheat the oven to 400°F/gas mark 6 (200°C).

Slice ½ inch (1 cm) off the top of the garlic bulb to expose the cloves then place cut side down on a baking tray. Drizzle with a little of the olive oil and roast for 30–35 minutes or until softened. Remove from the oven and set aside to cool.

Melt the coconut oil or ghee in a large saucepan over medium heat. Add the diced onion and thyme leaves and cook for 5 minutes or until the onion has softened. Add the lamb and cook, stirring frequently, for 3–4 minutes or until lamb is browned.

Add the broth, peas, spinach and apple cider vinegar. Bring to a boil, add the parsley, setting aside a little to use as a garnish, then reduce the heat to low and simmer, partially covered, for 5 minutes (or 15 minutes for a stronger flavor). Squeeze the roasted garlic cloves out of their skins and into the soup.

Remove from the heat and allow to cool slightly, then purée in a food processor or blender (remove some peas first to use as a garnish if you like). Season to taste, reheat slightly if necessary, and serve with a sprinkle of fresh parsley, a drizzle of olive oil and perhaps a garnish of peas.

GRANDMA'S CHICKEN SOUP

▲GF ▲WF ▲DF ▲SF

SERVES 4

This immune-boosting soup is the perfect comfort food on a chilly night.
If you're further advanced with your gut healing, try this soup unblended.

  ¼ cup (2 fl oz/60 ml) extra virgin olive oil
  3 cloves garlic, sliced
  1 onion, chopped
  2 teaspoons ground turmeric
  1 heaping teaspoon ground cumin
  1 heaping teaspoon sumac
  1 heaping teaspoon sweet paprika
  ½ cup (1¾ oz/50 g) almond meal
  6–8 skinless organic chicken thigh fillets
  2 cups chopped green vegetables (e.g. bok choy,
     zucchini, scallions, spinach)
  2 large mushrooms, sliced
  2 tablespoons (40 ml) apple cider vinegar
  2 tablespoons wheat-free tamari
  2 tablespoons (40 ml) lemon juice
  4 cups (35 fl oz/1 L) chicken broth (see page 146)
  Celtic sea salt and freshly cracked black pepper, to taste
  2 sprigs thyme

Preheat the oven to 325°F/gas mark 3 (170°C).

Heat 1 tablespoon (20 ml) of the oil in a flameproof casserole dish over medium
heat. Add the garlic and onion and cook for 3–4 minutes or until browned.
Leave in the casserole dish and set aside.

Combine the spices and almond meal on a plate. Roll the chicken thighs in the
spice mixture to cover. Heat the remaining oil in a frying pan over medium heat.
Add the chicken and brown on both sides, then transfer to the casserole dish
with the onion and garlic. Add the remaining ingredients except the thyme and
seasoning, then bring to a boil. Reduce the heat and simmer for 5 minutes.

Add the thyme, reserving a little as a garnish, and salt. Transfer the casserole
dish to the oven and bake for 30 minutes or until the chicken is cooked and
tender. Allow to cool slightly, then purée in a food processor or blender until
smooth. Grind on pepper, garnish with thyme and serve.

MARKET-FRESH VEGETABLE SOUP

▲ GF ▲ WF ▲ DF ▲ SF ▲ VEG

SERVES 6

This freezer-friendly soup is great to make in batches, and is best cooked using veggies at their freshest. It will flood your system with easily digestible nutrients along with the fiber you need to feed a healthy bacterial colony.

2 tablespoons (40 ml) extra virgin coconut oil or
   1 tablespoon (20 ml) ghee
1 leek, white part only, chopped
1 onion, diced
3 cloves garlic, crushed
3 stalks celery, diced
1 inch (2.5 cm) piece of ginger, peeled and grated
2/3 cup (5½ oz/160 g) sugar-free tomato paste
14 oz (400 g) can additive-free chopped tomatoes
5½ oz (150 g) green beans, topped, tailed and cut
   into 1¼–1½ inch (3–4 cm) lengths
½ cauliflower, roughly chopped
2 zucchini, diced
1 red pepper, seeded and diced
1 green pepper, seeded and diced
1 bunch (1 lb/450 g) kale, chopped
1 cup (1½ oz/45 g) spinach leaves, chopped
4 cups (35 fl oz/1 L) vegetable stock (see page 151)
   or filtered water, plus extra water as needed
1 handful of mixed herbs (e.g. flat-leaf [Italian] parsley, basil), chopped
freshly cracked black pepper, to taste
nutritional yeast flakes (optional), to serve
watercress leaves, to serve

Melt the oil or ghee in a large saucepan over medium heat. Add the leek, onion, garlic, celery and ginger and cook, stirring regularly, for 5 minutes or until lightly browned.

Stir in the tomato paste and chopped tomatoes, then cook for another 1–2 minutes. Add the beans, cauliflower, zucchini, peppers, kale and spinach, then cook, stirring frequently, for another 1–2 minutes.

continued on page 160

←··· continued

Add the stock or water and, if necessary, extra filtered water to cover the vegetables. Bring to a boil, then reduce the heat to low and simmer for 10–15 minutes or until the vegetables are tender. Add the herbs and stir to combine.

Remove from the heat and allow to cool slightly, then purée in a food processor or blender to your desired consistency.

Serve hot, sprinkled with black pepper, yeast flakes, if using, and watercress.

ANTI-INFLAMMATORY CAULI SOUP

▲GF ▲WF ▲DF ▲SF

SERVES 4

I love that a humble bouquet of white florets can deliver all the satisfaction of a starchy potato without feeding a colony of hungry candida. This soup is a beautiful light lunch option with the added benefits of anti-inflammatory spices and coconut milk to promote healthy gut flora.

1 tablespoon (20 ml) extra virgin coconut oil or 2 teaspoons ghee
1 onion, chopped
3 cloves garlic, crushed
2 teaspoons finely chopped ginger
2 teaspoons ground turmeric
2 teaspoons ground cumin
2 teaspoons curry powder
1 large cauliflower, roughly chopped
2 cups (17 fl oz/500 ml) vegetable stock (see page 151)
½ cup (4 fl oz/125 ml) additive-free coconut milk
Celtic sea salt and freshly cracked black pepper, to taste
chopped cilantro or scallion, to serve

Melt the oil or ghee in a large saucepan over medium heat. Add the onion and fry for 3–4 minutes or until browned. Add the garlic, ginger, turmeric, cumin and curry powder, and stir for 1 minute or until fragrant. Add the cauliflower, stock and coconut milk, then bring to a boil.

Reduce the heat to low and simmer, covered, for 30 minutes.

Remove from the heat and allow to cool slightly, then purée in a food processor or blender, in batches, if you prefer a smoother consistency. Add salt to taste, then garnish with black pepper and cilantro or scallions, and serve.

AVOCADO AND ALMOND SOUP

▲GF ▲WF ▲DF ▲SF ▲VEG

SERVES 4

This Mexican-style delight overshadows the wimpy conventional taco in a way that'll have your amigos favoring your dinner table. If you're craving a greasy takeout meal, this soup will hit the spot. It's big on flavor but soothing enough to allow the gut to do its healing work.

2 tablespoons (40 ml) extra virgin olive oil or butter
1 onion, chopped
2 ripe avocados, pitted and peeled
3–4 cups (26–35 fl oz/750 ml–1 L) vegetable stock
   (see page 151)
½ cup (4 fl oz/125 ml) almond milk (see page 123)
grated zest and juice of 1 lemon
1 teaspoon sweet paprika
½ teaspoon ground cumin
pinch of cayenne pepper
1 clove garlic, crushed
Celtic sea salt and freshly cracked black pepper, to taste
cilantro, to serve
lime quarters, to serve

Heat the oil or butter in a medium saucepan over medium heat. Add the onion and cook for 3–4 minutes or until browned. Transfer the cooked onion to a food processor, add all the remaining ingredients except the pepper, cilantro and lime, and process until smooth. Chill until ready to serve. Grind on pepper, garnish with cilantro, and serve with the lime quarters.

SWEET GREEN BEAN SOUP

▲GF ▲WF ▲DF ▲SF ▲VEG

SERVES 4

Green beans, like their fellow legume family members – peanuts, lentils, peas and dried beans – are high in calcium, potassium and B vitamins, but are much more easily digestible and belly-friendly.

2 tablespoons (40 ml) extra virgin coconut oil or 1 tablespoon (20 ml) ghee
1 onion, diced
2 cloves garlic, crushed
2 stalks celery, chopped
1 turnip, peeled and sliced
1 lb 2 oz (500 g) green beans, trimmed
4 cups (35 fl oz/1 L) vegetable stock (see page 151)
1 cup (9 fl oz/250 ml) additive-free coconut milk
pinch of Celtic sea salt
freshly cracked black pepper, to taste

Melt the oil or ghee in a medium saucepan over medium heat. Add the onion, garlic, celery and turnip, and cook, stirring occasionally, for 10 minutes or until softened. Add the green beans and cook for another 5–10 minutes.

Pour in the stock and bring to a boil, then reduce the heat and simmer, covered, for 30 minutes or until the beans are cooked through.

Stir in the coconut milk, reserving a little to serve, and heat for a few minutes, then remove from the heat and allow to cool slightly. Add salt and purée in a food processor or blender until the consistency is to your liking. Reheat gently if necessary, drizzle with reserved coconut milk, grind on black pepper and serve.

WATERCRESS, LEEK AND COCONUT SOUP

▲GF ▲WF ▲DF ▲SF ▲VEG

SERVES 2

Watercress has been shown to reduce DNA damage in white blood cells and positively alter blood antioxidant concentrations, making it a wonderful medicinal plant to decrease inflammation and detoxify your entire body. Enjoy its fresh, earthy taste in this well-balanced, creamy blend.

1 tablespoon (20 ml) extra virgin coconut oil or 2 teaspoons ghee
1 onion, diced
1 clove garlic, crushed
1 leek, white part only, finely sliced
1 medium turnip, peeled and diced
2¾ cups (3 oz/85 g) watercress, rinsed, plus extra to serve
9½ fl oz (270 ml) can additive-free coconut milk
1½ cups (13 fl oz/375 ml) vegetable stock (see page 151)
Celtic sea salt and freshly cracked black pepper, to taste

Melt the oil or ghee in a medium saucepan over medium heat. Add the onion and garlic and cook, stirring frequently, for 3–4 minutes or until transparent. Add the leek, turnip, watercress, coconut milk and stock, then bring to a boil. Reduce the heat to low then simmer, covered, for 20 minutes.

Remove from the heat and allow to cool slightly, then purée in a food processor or blender until smooth. Add salt to taste, reheat if necessary, then grind on black pepper, garnish with extra watercress and serve.

SUPER GREEN SOUP

▲GF ▲WF ▲DF ▲SF ▲VEG

SERVES 2–3

The alkalizing, detoxifying, cancer-fighting and circulation-boosting properties
of green vegetables make them a high priority on the list of gut-healing foods.
Cooking this super soup lightly softens the cell walls of the greens, allowing
your digestive tract to tolerate all those precious nutrients easily.

> 1 tablespoon (20 ml) extra virgin olive oil
> 1 onion, chopped
> 1 leek, white part only, chopped
> 3 cloves garlic, crushed
> 2 stalks celery, sliced
> 2 bunches (14 oz/400 g) broccolini, chopped
> 1 bunch (1 lb/450 g) kale, chopped
> 2 cups (17 fl oz/500 ml) vegetable stock (see page 151)
> 9½ fl oz (270 ml) can additive-free coconut milk
> 2 tablespoons (40 ml) lemon juice
> Celtic sea salt and freshly cracked black pepper, to taste
> nutritional yeast flakes, to serve

Heat the oil in a large saucepan over medium heat. Add the onion, leek, garlic
and celery and cook, stirring frequently, for 5 minutes or until softened.

Add the broccolini and kale and cook, stirring frequently, for another
5 minutes. Add the stock and coconut milk, bring to a boil, then reduce
the heat and simmer for 15–20 minutes.

Remove from the heat and allow to cool slightly, then purée in a food
processor or blender. Reheat gently, then add the lemon juice and season
to taste. Serve sprinkled with yeast flakes.

CELERY, LEEK AND THYME SOUP

▲GF ▲WF ▲DF ▲SF ▲VEG

SERVES 4

Although not as well known as their famous counterparts, onions and garlic, leeks are significant vegetables in the fight against chronic low-level inflammatory states, including diabetes, obesity and rheumatoid arthritis. Leeks can decrease your risk of developing these conditions by virtue of their polyphenol content.

1 tablespoon (20 ml) extra virgin olive oil
4 cloves garlic, sliced
1 leek, white part only, chopped
1½ heads celery, cut into ¼ inch (5 mm) slices
2 cardamom pods, seeds only, pods discarded
1 teaspoon dried thyme
4 cups (35 fl oz/1 L) vegetable stock (see page 151)
⅔ cup (3¾ oz/105 g) natural cashews,
   pre-soaked (see page 120) and drained
½ cup (4 fl oz/125 ml) additive-free coconut milk

Heat the oil in a large saucepan over medium heat. Add the garlic and leek and cook for 3–4 minutes or until soft. Add the celery, cardamom seeds and thyme and cook for another 5 minutes.

Add the stock and bring to a boil, then reduce the heat and simmer, covered, for 20–25 minutes or until the celery is tender.

Remove from the heat and allow to cool slightly, then add the cashews. Purée in a food processor or blender until smooth. Return to the saucepan, add the coconut milk and warm through before serving.

WHITE FISH SOUP WITH SAFFRON

▲GF ▲WF ▲DF ▲SF

SERVES 4

This beautifully light and flavorful soup has a dose of precious saffron, which has been used as a versatile medicine since ancient times. A foundation of fish stock will offer your body an array of essential minerals.

> 2 tablespoons (40 ml) extra virgin olive oil
> 1 onion, chopped
> 2 stalks celery, chopped
> 1 leek, white part only, chopped
> 1 medium fennel bulb, fronds reserved, bulb chopped
> 3 cloves garlic, crushed
> juice of ½ lemon
> grated zest of 1 lemon
> 14 oz (400 g) can additive-free chopped tomatoes
> 1 small red pepper, seeded and chopped
> pinch of saffron threads
> 2 sprigs thyme
> 4 cups (35 fl oz/1 L) vegetable stock
>   (see page 151) or fish stock
> pinch of cayenne pepper
> 14 oz (400 g) boneless white fish fillets,
>   whole or roughly chopped
> ½ teaspoon Celtic sea salt
> 2 tablespoons nutritional yeast flakes (optional)
> pinch of freshly cracked black pepper

Heat the oil in a medium saucepan over medium heat. Add the onion, celery, leek, chopped fennel and garlic, and cook for 3-4 minutes or until soft. Add the lemon juice and zest, tomato, pepper, saffron and thyme, reserving a little of the thyme to use as a garnish. Cook for 2-3 minutes, then add the stock and cayenne pepper. Bring to a boil, then reduce the heat and simmer for 25-30 minutes. Add the fish and simmer for another 10 minutes.

Remove from the heat and allow to cool slightly, then purée in a food processor or blender until smooth. (Alternatively, purée the soup before adding the fish.) Add the salt to taste, reheat if necessary, then serve sprinkled with yeast flakes, if using, and black pepper, and garnished with reserved fennel fronds and thyme.

SUMMER HERB SOUP

▲GF ▲WF ▲DF ▲SF ▲VEG

SERVES 4

This bright, fresh soup (pictured on page 174) celebrates the bounty of herbs that burst forth from the soil in the warmer seasons, such as sage. Vibrantly nourishing, it's full of volatile plant oils that will keep bad bacteria and yeasts at bay.

> 2 tablespoons (40 ml) extra virgin coconut oil or 1 tablespoon (20 ml) ghee
> 1 onion
> 3 cloves garlic, crushed
> ½ medium cauliflower, cut into florets
> 4 cups (35 fl oz/1 L) vegetable stock (see page 151)
> 9½ fl oz (270 ml) can additive-free coconut milk
> 2 cups fresh herbs (e.g. basil, flat-leaf [Italian] parsley, sage, chives, dill, tarragon), finely chopped
> 4 sprigs thyme
> 1 small handful of watercress, roughly chopped
> 1 cup (1½ oz/40 g) roughly chopped spinach
> 1 tablespoon (20 ml) lemon juice
> Celtic sea salt and freshly cracked black pepper, to taste
> pinch of nutmeg

Melt the oil or ghee in a medium saucepan over medium heat. Add the onion and cook, stirring frequently, for 3–4 minutes or until translucent, then add the garlic and cook for 1–2 minutes. Add the cauliflower and cook, stirring frequently, for 5 minutes or until browned.

Add the stock and bring to a boil, then add the coconut milk and simmer for 2–3 minutes. Add the herbs, watercress, spinach and lemon juice, then reduce the heat to very low and simmer, partially covered, for 10 minutes. Be careful not to let the mixture boil.

Season to taste and add the nutmeg. Remove from the heat and allow to cool slightly, then purée in a food processor or blender to your desired consistency. Serve warm.

L–R: Comforting Cauli and Turnip Soup (page 194); Summer Herb Soup (page 172); Iceberg Lettuce and Coconut Soup

ICEBERG LETTUCE AND COCONUT SOUP

▲GF ▲WF ▲DF ▲SF ▲VEG

SERVES 4

This perfect midsummer meal is light and easy on the digestive system, and fresh and speedy to prepare. Lettuce is magically transformed into a bowl of deliciousness with creamy and rounded flavors.

> 1 tablespoon (20 ml) extra virgin coconut oil or 2 teaspoons ghee
> 2 cloves garlic, crushed
> 1 onion, chopped
> 4 cups (35 fl oz/1 L) vegetable stock (see page 151)
> 1 head iceberg lettuce, roughly chopped
> 1 teaspoon Celtic sea salt
> freshly cracked black pepper, to taste
> ¼ cup (2 fl oz/60 ml) additive-free coconut milk
> flat-leaf (Italian) parsley, to serve

Melt the oil or ghee in a medium saucepan over medium heat. Add the garlic and onion and cook, stirring frequently, for 2–3 minutes or until starting to soften. Add the stock, bring to a boil, then reduce the heat to low and simmer for 5 minutes.

Add the lettuce and simmer for 10 minutes or until the lettuce is soft.

Add the salt and pepper to taste. Stir through the coconut milk, then purée in a food processor or blender to your desired consistency. Reheat gently if necessary, garnish with parsley, then serve.

KARMIC KORMA

▲GF ▲WF ▲DF ▲SF ▲VEG

SERVES 4

Alluring and grounding, this spice-dusted blend of creamy coconut, cashews and vegetables (pictured on page 179) is definitely one to eat mindfully. Imagine every spoonful bringing nourishment and healing to your body.

⅔ cup (3¾ oz/105 g) natural cashews
1 tablespoon (6 g) ground coriander
3 teaspoons curry powder
2 teaspoons ground turmeric
1 teaspoon ground cardamom
1 teaspoon red chili flakes
¾ teaspoon ground fennel
¼ teaspoon ground cinnamon
14 fl oz (400 ml) can additive-free coconut milk
1½ tablespoons (30 ml) extra virgin coconut oil or 3 teaspoons ghee
1 onion, chopped
4 cloves garlic, crushed
1 inch (2.5 cm) piece of ginger, peeled and grated
1 large tomato, diced
½ medium cauliflower, cut into florets
1 large turnip, peeled and diced
1 cup (5½ oz/150 g) green peas (fresh or frozen)
1 cup (9 fl oz/250 ml) filtered water
Celtic sea salt and freshly cracked black pepper, to taste
1 handful of fresh cilantro leaves (optional), to serve

Soak the cashews in hot filtered water for 30 minutes. Drain.

Combine the spices in a small bowl and set aside.

Pulse the cashews with the coconut milk in a food processor until smooth.

Melt the oil or ghee in a large saucepan over medium-high heat. Add the onion, garlic and ginger and cook, stirring frequently, for 3-4 minutes or until starting to soften.

Add the spices and cook, stirring frequently, for 1 minute or until the spices are aromatic. Add the tomato and cook, stirring frequently, for another 1 minute. Add the remaining vegetables, the water and the cashew mixture, then stir to combine and cook for another 10 minutes. Add a little more filtered water if necessary.

Reduce the heat to low and cook for 35 minutes, adding more filtered water if the sauce starts to reduce too much.

Remove from the heat and season to taste, then allow to cool slightly. Purée in a food processor or blender until smooth. Serve sprinkled with cilantro leaves.

LEMONGRASS THAI SOUP

▲GF ▲WF ▲DF ▲SF ▲VEG

SERVES 4

Thai cuisine is a kaleidoscopic treasure chest of medicinal herbs and spices. The plant oils of lemongrass in particular have been shown to inhibit multi-resistant strains of bacteria and yeast, making it a must-have ingredient for strong immunity.

3 cups (26 fl oz/750 ml) vegetable stock
3¼ inch (8 cm) piece of galangal, peeled and grated
2 stalks lemongrass, cut into 2 inch (5 cm) pieces
3–4 kaffir lime leaves, torn
4 scallions, sliced
7 drops liquid stevia
9½ fl oz (270 ml) can additive-free coconut milk
1 tablespoon (20 ml) apple cider vinegar
2 tablespoons (30 g) wheat-free tamari
1 red pepper, seeded and sliced
1 cup (2½ oz/70 g) mushrooms, quartered
¼ cup (2 fl oz/60 ml) lime juice
grated zest of 1 lime
freshly cracked black pepper, to taste
cilantro leaves, to serve

Bring the vegetable stock, galangal, lemongrass, kaffir lime leaves, scallions and stevia to a boil in a large saucepan over medium heat. Reduce the heat to low and simmer for 5 minutes.

Stir through the coconut milk, vinegar and tamari, then simmer for 10 minutes. Add the pepper and mushroom and simmer for another 5 minutes.

Remove from the heat. Take out the lemongrass and lime leaves. Add the lime juice and zest, then purée in a food processor or blender until smooth. Serve with a grind of black pepper, garnished with cilantro.

L–R: *KarmicKorma (page 176)*;
Lemongrass Thai Soup

L–R: Bok Choy and Mushroom Soup;
Delectable Detox Soup (page 182)

BOK CHOY AND MUSHROOM SOUP

▲ GF ▲ WF ▲ DF ▲ SF ▲ VEG

SERVES 2–3

There won't be "mushroom" for dessert after a bowl of this substantial aromatic and hearty broth. This spruced-up soup using bountiful bok choy is deeply nourishing and mineral-rich.

1 tablespoon (20 ml) extra virgin olive oil or extra virgin coconut oil
2 cloves garlic, crushed
2 tablespoons (15 g) grated ginger
8 baby bok choy, cut in half lengthwise, then washed and roughly chopped
6 cups (52 fl oz/1.5 L) vegetable broth (see page 151)
2 cups (6¼ oz/180 g) button mushrooms, sliced
¼ cup (2 fl oz/60 ml) wheat-free tamari
¼ cup (2 fl oz/60 ml) apple cider vinegar
1 cup (2½ oz/75 g) sugar snap peas, strings removed, plus extra to serve
Celtic sea salt and freshly cracked black pepper, to taste

Heat the oil in a large saucepan over medium heat. Add the garlic and ginger and cook for 2–3 minutes or until soft. Add the bok choy and cook for 2–3 minutes or until wilted.

Add the remaining ingredients, except the salt and pepper, and bring to a boil, then reduce the heat and simmer, covered, for 15 minutes. Season to taste.

Remove from the heat and allow to cool slightly, then purée in a food processor or blender to your desired consistency. Serve garnished with opened sugar snap pea pods.

SUPERCHARGED TIP

For a creamy soup add 1 cup (9 fl oz/250 ml) additive-free coconut milk or almond milk (see page 123).

DELECTABLE DETOX SOUP

▲GF ▲WF ▲DF ▲SF ▲VEG

SERVES 4

Sweep your insides clean with this blend of highly alkalizing and blood-oxygenating green vegetables, yeast-busting onions and hearty herbs (pictured on page 180). Its high fiber and chlorophyll content will draw the toxins out of your digestive tract and leave you feeling as clean as a whistle.

1 tablespoon (20 ml) extra virgin coconut oil or 2 teaspoons ghee
1 onion, chopped
1 leek, white part only, sliced
2 cloves garlic, chopped
3 cups (26 fl oz/750 ml) broth or stock of your choice (see pages 146–51)
1 lb 2 oz (500 g) assorted green vegetables (e.g. broccoli, spinach, zucchini, celery), roughly chopped
1 small bunch (2 oz/55 g) flat-leaf (Italian) parsley, chopped
grated zest of 1 lemon
2 tablespoons (40 ml) apple cider vinegar
2 teaspoons freshly grated ginger
1 bunch (2½ oz/75 g) cilantro, chopped, plus extra to serve
¼ teaspoon freshly cracked black pepper

Melt the oil or ghee in a medium saucepan over medium heat. Add the onion, leek and garlic and cook, stirring frequently, for 3–4 minutes or until softened.

Add the broth or stock and vegetables, then bring to a boil. Reduce the heat to low, then add the remaining ingredients and simmer, covered, for 15 minutes.

Remove from the heat and allow to cool slightly, then purée in a food processor or blender to your desired consistency. Serve warm, garnished with extra cilantro.

SUPER-QUICK CHICKEN SOUP

▲GF ▲WF ▲DF ▲SF

SERVES 2

This one-pot meal is the cheat's version of a bowl full of nourishment, and outshines any supermarket version. The twist of zingy lime will keep you on your toes and have an alkalizing effect on your digestive tract.

1 tablespoon (20 ml) extra virgin coconut oil
2 cloves garlic, crushed
1 French shallot, peeled and chopped
1 inch (2.5 cm) piece of ginger, grated
2 stalks lemongrass, white part only, chopped
9½ fl oz (270 ml) can additive-free coconut milk,
  plus extra to serve (optional)
2 cups (17 fl oz/500 ml) chicken broth (see page 146)
grated zest and juice of 1 lime, plus extra lime juice
  to serve (optional)
1 tablespoon (20 ml) apple cider vinegar
2 tablespoons (30 g) wheat-free tamari
Celtic sea salt and freshly cracked black pepper, to taste

Melt the oil in a heavy-based medium saucepan over medium heat. Add the garlic, shallot, ginger and lemongrass and cook for 3 minutes or until soft.

Add the coconut milk and chicken broth. Bring to a boil, then reduce the heat to low and simmer for 5 minutes.

Add the lime zest and juice, vinegar and tamari. Season to taste and serve with extra lime juice and coconut milk, if desired.

FENNEL, TOMATO AND ROAST GARLIC SOUP

▲ GF ▲ WF ▲ DF ▲ SF ▲ VEG

SERVES 2-3

Fennel is seriously underrated. Don't be put off by its blandly colored bulbousness; once it's roasted, a miraculous alchemy occurs, bringing out the most scrumptious caramelized flavors. Fennel is also full of phytochemicals that act as antioxidants, fighting free radicals.

> 1 bulb garlic, whole, unpeeled
> 1 tablespoon (20 ml) extra virgin olive oil, plus extra for drizzling
> Celtic sea salt, to taste
> 1 large bulb fennel, fronds reserved, bulb diced
> ½ cup (4½ oz/125 g) sugar-free tomato paste
> 14 oz (400 g) can additive-free chopped tomatoes
> 5 cups (44 fl oz/1.25 L) vegetable stock (see page 151)
> 1 tablespoon (20 ml) apple cider vinegar
> ¼ cup (2 fl oz/60 ml) lemon juice
> freshly cracked black pepper, to taste

Preheat the oven to 400°F/gas mark 6 (200°C).

Slice ½ inch (1 cm) off the top of the garlic bulb to expose the cloves, then place cut side down on a baking tray. Drizzle with a little olive oil and sprinkle with salt. Roast for 30 minutes or until softened, then remove from the oven and set aside to cool. Once cool enough to handle, squeeze the garlic cloves out of their skins into a small bowl.

Heat the oil in a medium saucepan over medium heat, then add the fennel with a pinch of salt. Cook, stirring frequently, for 20 minutes or until deep brown and caramelized.

Add the tomato paste, tomato and roast garlic flesh, then cook for another 6 minutes, stirring frequently. Add the stock and stir to combine, then bring to a boil and simmer, partially covered, for 15 minutes.

Remove from the heat and add the vinegar and lemon juice. Allow to cool slightly, then purée in a food processor or blender until smooth. Grind on pepper, garnish with reserved fennel fronds and serve.

SALMON CHOWDER

▲GF ▲WF ▲DF ▲SF

SERVES 4

Chow down on this chowder to experience the gut-healing effects of wild-caught salmon. The fatty acids in salmon have been linked with protection against several gastrointestinal diseases, through their anti-inflammatory activity and their ability to boost healthy microorganisms in the gut.

1 tablespoon (20 ml) extra virgin coconut oil
4 salmon fillets (skin and bones removed)
½ onion, diced
2 cloves garlic, chopped
1 stalk celery, diced
½ teaspoon curry powder
4 cups (35 fl oz/1 L) chicken broth (see page 146)
2 turnips, peeled and cut into 1 inch (2.5 cm) cubes
1 teaspoon dried parsley
1 cup (9 fl oz/250 ml) additive-free coconut milk
Celtic sea salt and freshly cracked black pepper, to taste
fresh flat-leaf (Italian) parsley, to serve

Melt half the coconut oil in a large frying pan over medium heat. Add the salmon and cook for 3 minutes on each side or until just cooked. Set aside until cool enough to handle, then flake into pieces.

Melt the remaining oil in a large saucepan over medium heat. Add the onion, garlic, celery and curry powder, and cook, stirring frequently, for 3–4 minutes or until the onion is translucent. Add the broth, turnip and parsley and cook, covered, for 20 minutes or until the turnip is soft.

Add the coconut milk and stir to combine, then remove from the heat and allow to cool slightly. Transfer to a food processor or blender with the flaked salmon and purée until smooth. (Alternatively, purée the soup before adding the fish.) Season to taste, garnish with fresh parsley and serve.

THIRTY-CLOVE GARLIC AND ONION SOUP

▲GF ▲WF ▲SF

SERVES 3–4

Garlic is one of the most powerful medicinal foods. Its anti-inflammatory, anti-parasitic, antibiotic and antiviral properties make it an incredibly important ingredient in the defence against digestive assaults of all varieties. Load up on garlic's goodness with this bold and flavorful soup.

3 bulbs garlic, whole, unpeeled
2 tablespoons (40 ml) extra virgin olive oil
2 tablespoons (28 g) unsalted butter
1 large onion, finely chopped
4 cups (35 fl oz/1 L) vegetable stock or chicken broth
  (see pages 151 and 146)
½ teaspoon ground turmeric
½ teaspoon ground cumin
¼ cup (2 fl oz/60 ml) apple cider vinegar
1 tablespoon (15 g) wheat-free tamari
1 tablespoon (20 ml) lemon juice
Celtic sea salt and freshly cracked black pepper, to taste
1 teaspoon dried mixed herbs such as oregano, thyme
  and sage (optional)
¼ cup (2 fl oz/60 ml) additive-free coconut milk (optional)
fresh herbs, to serve

Preheat the oven to 345°F/gas mark 5 (175°C).

Slice ½ inch (1 cm) off the top of each garlic bulb to expose the cloves, then place cut side down on a baking tray. Drizzle with the olive oil, then roast for 45 minutes. Remove from the oven and set aside to cool. Once cool enough to handle, squeeze the garlic cloves out of their skins into the bowl of a food processor. Pulse for a few seconds, then set aside.

Meanwhile, heat the butter in a large saucepan over medium heat. Add the onion and cook, stirring frequently, for 5 minutes or until translucent. Add the stock or broth, turmeric, cumin, vinegar, tamari, lemon juice, blended garlic, salt, pepper and herbs, if using, then bring to a boil. Reduce the heat to low–medium, then simmer, covered, for 30 minutes.

For a creamier soup, add the coconut milk before serving and heat through. Serve garnished with fresh herbs.

CREAMY MUSHROOM SOUP

▲GF ▲WF ▲DF ▲SF ▲VEG

SERVES 4

Mushrooms are highly medicinal, protecting against inflammation and keeping your immune system fighting strong. This sophisticated, silky-textured soup makes a filling lunch or dinner. If you have candida, avoid this soup until your gut has improved.

1 tablespoon (20 ml) extra virgin olive oil
1 onion, finely diced
2 cloves garlic, finely chopped
2 large carrots, cut into ½ inch (1 cm) dice
1 tablespoon (2 g) chopped rosemary, plus extra sprigs to serve
1 teaspoon Celtic sea salt
freshly cracked black pepper, to taste
1 lb 10 oz (750 g) button mushrooms, sliced
5 cups (44 fl oz/1.25 L) vegetable stock (see page 151)
2 tablespoons (30 g) wheat-free tamari
1 tablespoon (20 ml) apple cider vinegar
2 tablespoons (40 ml) puréed tomatoes
1 cup (9 fl oz/250 ml) additive-free coconut milk
2 tablespoons (25 g) nutritional yeast flakes, to serve

Heat the oil in a large saucepan over medium heat. Add the onion, garlic, carrot, rosemary, salt and pepper and cook, stirring frequently, for 5–6 minutes or until the carrot is starting to soften. Add the mushroom and cook for another 5 minutes.

Add the stock, tamari, vinegar, tomatoes and coconut milk. Stir to combine, then bring to a simmer and cook for 15–20 minutes or until the carrot is cooked.

Remove from the heat and allow to cool slightly, then purée in a food processor or blender until smooth. (If you prefer a chunkier soup, omit this step.) Serve topped with yeast flakes and garnished with extra rosemary.

FLIRTY FRENCH ONION SOUP

▲GF ▲WF ▲DF ▲SF ▲VEG

SERVES 4

Easy on the digestive system and even easier on the wallet, this soup is a great one to make with leftover onions and herbs, and is really simple to throw together. Don't let an onion's cheapness deter you from flirting with these darlings in the kitchen. When caramelized, they're refined and sweet, and will protect your tummy from inflammation and yeasts.

> 2 tablespoons (40 ml) olive oil
> 8 onions, thinly sliced
> 3 cloves garlic, finely chopped
> 8 cups (68 fl oz/2 L) chicken broth (see page 146)
> 2 tablespoons (30 g) wheat-free tamari
> 2 tablespoons (40 ml) apple cider vinegar
> Celtic sea salt and freshly cracked black pepper, to taste
> 1 handful of fresh chives (optional), chopped, to serve

Heat the olive oil in a large saucepan over medium heat. Add the onion and garlic and cook, stirring frequently, for 8–10 minutes or until the onion has softened and caramelized.

Add the broth, tamari and vinegar and bring to a boil. Reduce the heat to low, then simmer, covered, for 30 minutes.

Season to taste and serve sprinkled with the chopped chives, if using.

SUPERCHARGED TIP

Onions provide significant health benefits, reducing cholesterol and attacking bacteria that cause infection. If you're following a low-FODMAP diet, give this recipe a wide berth, unless you know onions don't affect your digestion.

COMFORTING CAULI AND TURNIP SOUP

▲GF ▲WF ▲DF ▲SF ▲VEG

SERVES 4

Turnips and cauliflower are two of my favorite replacements for starchy potatoes, and they're great for healing inflammation, as well as detoxification and digestion. They're also high in antioxidants and rich in vitamins and minerals, all of which are vital to restoring gut health. The two vegetables combine in this velvety soup (pictured on page 174) to provide the satisfaction of carbs in a gut-friendly manner.

2 tablespoons (40 ml) extra virgin coconut oil or extra virgin olive oil, or 1 tablespoon (20 ml) ghee
1 large onion, chopped
3 stalks celery, chopped
2 cloves garlic, crushed
1 cauliflower, roughly chopped
2 small round turnips, peeled and chopped
1½ inch (4 cm) piece of ginger, peeled and roughly chopped
2 tablespoons (25 g) nutritional yeast flakes
1 handful of flat-leaf (Italian) parsley
3 cups (26 fl oz/750 ml) chicken broth or vegetable stock (see pages 146 and 151)
1½ teaspoons Celtic sea salt
¼ teaspoon freshly cracked black pepper

Heat the oil or ghee in a medium saucepan. Add the onion, celery and garlic and stir to coat with oil before adding the cauliflower and turnip. Cook, stirring frequently, for 10 minutes.

Add the ginger, yeast flakes, parsley and broth or stock, then bring to a boil. Stir a couple of times, then reduce the heat and simmer, covered, for 20 minutes. Add salt and pepper.

Remove from the heat and allow to cool slightly, then purée in a food processor or blender. Reheat gently if necessary, then serve.

SUPERFOOD SOUP

▲GF ▲WF ▲DF ▲SF ▲VEG

SERVES 3–4

This nutrient-dense combination provides a cross-section of phytonutrients and antioxidants, including vitamin K, coenzyme Q10, folate, iron and the carotenoids – lutein and zeaxanthin – thanks to those chlorophyll-rich and detoxifying greens such as kale and spinach. It's a multivitamin dose packed into the comfort of a soup bowl.

  1 tablespoon (20 ml) extra virgin coconut oil or 2 teaspoons ghee
  1 onion, diced
  2 cloves garlic, crushed
  ½ teaspoon finely chopped ginger
  1 bunch (1 lb/450 g) kale, washed and stems removed
  1 cup (2¼ oz/60 g) broccoli, roughly chopped
  1 bunch (1 lb/450 g) spinach
  1 bunch (1 lb 5 oz/600 g) bok choy
  1 cup (5½ oz/155 g) diced butternut squash
  4 cups (35 fl oz/1 L) vegetable stock (see page 151)
  1 cup (9 fl oz/250 ml) additive-free coconut milk
  1 tablespoon (15 g) nutritional yeast flakes, to serve

Melt the oil or ghee in a large saucepan over medium heat. Add the onion and cook for 3–4 minutes or until translucent. Add the garlic, ginger and green vegetables and sweat for 3–4 minutes.

Add the squash and stock, then bring to a boil. Reduce the heat to low, pour in the coconut milk, then cook, covered, for another 20 minutes.

Remove from the heat and allow to cool slightly, then purée in a food processor or blender until smooth. Serve sprinkled with yeast flakes.

LAMB AND ZUCCHINI SOUP

▲GF ▲WF ▲DF ▲SF

SERVES 4

The anti-inflammatory spices turmeric and cinnamon assert themselves beautifully here against the boisterous lamb and sweet zucchini – two winning participants standing shoulder to shoulder to deliver enough protein and fiber to boost immunity and get your digestive system moving.

2 tablespoons (40 ml) extra virgin olive oil
2 lb 4 oz (1 kg) diced lamb (shoulder or leg), fat trimmed
1 onion, finely sliced
2 teaspoons ground turmeric
2 teaspoons ground ginger
2 teaspoons ground cinnamon
1 tablespoon harissa
2 medium zucchini, chopped
8 cups (68 fl oz/2 L) chicken broth (see page 146)
1 organic egg (optional)
1 large tomato, diced
2 cups (3¼ oz/90 g) baby spinach
juice of 1 lemon
1 bunch (2½ oz/75 g) cilantro, leaves picked, to serve
freshly cracked black pepper, to serve

Heat half the oil in a large frying pan over high heat. Add half the lamb and cook for 5 minutes, browning on all sides. Remove from the pan and set aside. Repeat with the remaining lamb, using the same oil.

Heat the remaining oil in a large saucepan over medium heat. Add the onion and cook, stirring frequently, for 5–6 minutes or until caramelized. Add the turmeric, ginger and cinnamon and cook for 1–2 minutes or until the spices are aromatic. Add the lamb and stir to coat in the spice mix. Add the harissa and zucchini and stir well. Pour in the broth and bring to a boil, then reduce the heat and simmer, covered, for 1 hour or until the lamb is tender.

In a cup, lightly whisk the egg, if using. Pour it into the soup mixture, stirring constantly. Add the tomato, spinach and lemon juice, and simmer for 5 minutes.

Remove from the heat, allow to cool slightly, then purée in batches in a food processor or blender. Grind on the pepper, garnish with cilantro and serve.

PARSLEY AND LEEK SOUP WITH LEMON

▲GF ▲WF ▲SF

SERVES 4

This delicate soup is perfect as a light meal or snack to keep you satisfied. Parsley is wonderful for reducing gas and aiding detoxification, while leeks offer the many gut-defending and immune-boosting properties of the onion family.

 1 tablespoon (14 g) unsalted butter or ghee
 3 leeks, white part only, cut into 5 mm (¼ inch) slices
 8 medium parsnips, peeled and chopped
 2 tablespoons (40 ml) extra virgin olive oil
 1 teaspoon Celtic sea salt
 ½ teaspoon ground turmeric
 4 cups (35 fl oz/1 L) chicken broth or vegetable stock
    (see pages 146 and 151)
 grated zest of 1 lemon
 1 tablespoon (20 ml) lemon juice
 1 tablespoon (20 ml) apple cider vinegar
 2 large handfuls of flat-leaf (Italian) parsley, chopped
 1 cup (9 fl oz/250 ml) additive-free coconut milk
 freshly cracked black pepper, to taste

Melt the butter or ghee in a large saucepan over medium heat. Add the leek and toss to coat well in the oil, then cook for 5–7 minutes or until soft.

Add the parsnip, olive oil, salt and turmeric and mix well. Add the broth or stock, lemon zest, juice and vinegar, then bring to a boil. Reduce the heat to low and simmer, covered, for 20 minutes or until the parsnip is tender.

Add the parsley, reserving a little to garnish, then remove from the heat and stir through the coconut milk. Purée in a food processor or blender until smooth. Sprinkle with the reserved parsley and black pepper, then serve.

BROCCOLINI, KALE AND MINT SOUP

▲GF ▲WF ▲DF ▲SF ▲VEG

SERVES 3–4

Here's another soup full of greens that will make your gut adore you. The mint acts as a carminative (gas-reducer) on the gut, which is perfect if you ever face any discomfort, wind or pain as a result of digestive issues.

1 tablespoon (20 ml) extra virgin olive oil
1 onion, chopped
1 leek, white part only, chopped
3 cloves garlic, crushed
2 stalks celery, sliced
2 bunches (14 oz/400 g) broccolini, chopped
1 bunch (1 lb/450 g) kale, stalks removed, leaves roughly chopped
2 cups (17 fl oz/500 ml) vegetable stock (see page 151)
9½ fl oz (270 ml) can additive-free coconut milk
1 small handful of mint leaves
2 tablespoons (40 ml) lemon juice
Celtic sea salt and freshly cracked black pepper, to taste
nutritional yeast flakes, to serve

Heat the olive oil in a medium saucepan over medium heat. Add the onion, leek, garlic and celery and cook, stirring frequently, for 4–5 minutes or until the vegetables are beginning to soften. Add the broccolini and kale and cook, stirring frequently, for 5 minutes.

Add the stock and coconut milk, then bring to a boil. Reduce the heat to low and simmer for 15 minutes. Stir through the mint.

Remove from the heat and allow to cool slightly, then purée in a food processor or blender until smooth. Reheat if necessary, then stir in the lemon juice and season to taste. Serve sprinkled with yeast flakes.

GARDEN-FRESH ASPARAGUS SOUP

▲GF ▲WF ▲SF

SERVES 4

I just love the healthy snap of a bright-green new-season asparagus stalk.
Enjoy their uniquely grassy, sweet flavor and their healthy-bacteria-boosting
proteins in this fresh and uplifting soup.

2 tablespoons (28 g) butter
2 tablespoons (40 ml) extra virgin olive oil, plus extra to serve
2 scallions, finely chopped, plus extra, curled in cold water, to serve
½ teaspoon curry powder
¼ teaspoon ground ginger
½ teaspoon ground turmeric
grated zest and juice of 1 lemon
2 medium turnips, peeled and diced
3 cups (26 fl oz/750 ml) vegetable stock (see page 151)
9½ fl oz (270 ml) can additive-free coconut milk
1 bunch (6 oz/175 g) asparagus, cut into 1.5 cm (⅝ inch) pieces
½ teaspoon Celtic sea salt
freshly cracked black pepper, to taste

Melt the butter with the oil in a large saucepan over medium heat. Add the
scallions and cook, stirring frequently, until soft. Add the curry powder, ginger,
turmeric, lemon zest, juice and turnip and cook, stirring frequently,
for 5 minutes.

Add the stock, coconut milk and asparagus, and simmer, partially covered,
for 15 minutes or until the turnip is tender, then add the salt.

Remove from the heat and allow to cool slightly, then purée the mixture
in batches in a food processor or blender until smooth. Reheat gently if
necessary, then drizzle with olive oil, grind on black pepper and garnish
with curled scallions.

CLEANSING CHICKEN AND GINGER SOUP

▲GF ▲WF ▲DF ▲SF

SERVES 4

Chicken and ginger are perfect partners in this fragrantly zesty bowl of invigorating medicinal goodness. Embraced warmly, it's the perfect antidote to an upset stomach and feelings of nausea.

1 tablespoon (20 ml) extra virgin coconut oil or 2 teaspoons ghee
1 onion, chopped
4 cloves garlic, crushed
1 tablespoon (7 g) ground turmeric
2 tablespoons (16 g) grated ginger
1 lb 2 oz (500 g) organic chicken breast, cut into small chunks
6 cups (52 fl oz/1.5 L) chicken broth or vegetable stock
   (see pages 146 and 151)
1 tablespoon (20 ml) apple cider vinegar
1 tablespoon (20 ml) sugar-free mustard
2 tablespoons (30 g) wheat-free tamari

Melt the oil or ghee in a large saucepan over medium heat. Add the onion, then cook for 3–4 minutes or until translucent. Add the garlic, turmeric, ginger and chicken and cook, stirring frequently, for 5 minutes or until the chicken is browned on all sides.

Add the broth or stock and bring to a boil, then reduce the heat and simmer for 10 minutes. Add the remaining ingredients and simmer for 5 minutes.

Remove from the heat and allow to cool slightly, then purée in a food processor or blender until smooth. Serve warm.

ZESTY ZUCCHINI SOUP

▲GF ▲WF ▲DF ▲SF

SERVES 4–6

If you face any blah feelings along the road to your vibrantly healthy gut, this soup will put the swing back in your step. With its zingy flavors and wholesome ingredients, you'll be surprised how thoroughly a formerly bland zucchini can satisfy your tastebuds.

1 tablespoon (20 g) extra virgin coconut oil
1 onion, chopped
1 teaspoon crushed garlic
2 teaspoons ground turmeric
½ teaspoon Celtic sea salt
pinch of freshly cracked black pepper
2 lb 4 oz (1 kg) zucchini, trimmed and chopped
3½ cups (30 fl oz/875 ml) beef or chicken broth (see pages 146–47)
grated zest of 1 lemon
2 tablespoons (40 ml) lemon juice
1 teaspoon apple cider vinegar
½ cup (4 fl oz/125 ml) additive-free coconut milk

Melt the oil in a medium saucepan over high heat. Add the onion and garlic, then cook, stirring frequently, for 3 minutes or until softened. Add the turmeric and seasoning, then cook, stirring constantly, for 30 seconds. Reduce the heat to medium and add the zucchini, then cook, stirring frequently, for 5–6 minutes or until the zucchini is beginning to soften.

Add the stock, zest, juice and vinegar and bring to a boil, then reduce the heat and simmer for 20 minutes or until the zucchini is very tender.

Remove from the heat and allow to cool a little, then purée in a food processor or blender. Return to the saucepan over low heat, then add the coconut milk and heat through before serving.

Easy-to-digest
meals in a bowl

Come and join me for breakfast with a bowl
of Creamy Buckwheat Porridge or scrumptious
Scrambled Eggs. Lunch on Sardine Mash Pot
or Savory Smashed Root Vegetables, or feast
at dinner with a Salmon and Broccoli
or Ratatouille Bowl. Pillowy, billowy comfort
food has never tasted or felt so good.

CHEESY MASHED CAULIFLOWER

▲GF ▲WF ▲DF ▲SF ▲VEG

SERVES 2

Using cauliflower creates a light fluffy mash without the gut-wrenching irritable bowel symptoms that accompany potato. Flavor up this mild-mannered mash with nutritional yeast for a cheesy taste and a burst of B vitamins.

    3 cups (13 oz/375 g) cauliflower florets
    1 tablespoon (12 g) nutritional yeast flakes
    1 tablespoon (14 g) almond butter
    1 teaspoon Celtic sea salt
    ½ teaspoon freshly cracked black pepper
    pinch of nutmeg
    1 tablespoon (20 ml) almond milk (see page 123), optional
    flat-leaf (Italian) parsley or micro parsley, to serve

Put the cauliflower in a steamer over a saucepan of boiling water and steam for 8–10 minutes or until soft. Remove from the heat and allow to cool slightly, then purée in a food processor with all the remaining ingredients except the almond milk until smooth. If the mixture is too thick, add the almond milk or a little filtered water.

Serve warm, garnished with parsley.

SALMON AND BROCCOLI BOWL

▲ GF   ▲ WF   ▲ DF   ▲ SF

SERVES 1

Why wreak havoc on your digestive system when you can enjoy easy-to-digest bowls of goodness? Load up on this warm and filling, perfectly nutritionally balanced comfort food. Broccoli adds fiber, and the good fats in salmon will help deliver much-needed nutrients straight to your belly.

> 1 small turnip, peeled and diced
> ½ head broccoli, cut into florets
> 3½ oz (100 g) fresh salmon fillet, skinned and deboned
> ½ cup (4 fl oz/125 ml) almond milk (see page 123)
> freshly cracked black pepper, to taste

Cook the turnip and broccoli in a saucepan of boiling water for 8–10 minutes or until tender. Drain and set aside.

Put the salmon in a small frying pan over medium heat and pour over the almond milk. Bring to a boil, then reduce the heat to low and simmer, covered, for 7 minutes or until the salmon is just cooked.

Place the salmon, with the almond milk it was cooked in, and the cooked vegetables in a food processor and pulse to your desired consistency. If you prefer a smoother consistency, add more almond milk. If you prefer a chunkier version, omit the processing step and simply mix everything together in a bowl, as illustrated opposite. Serve with a grind of black pepper.

CREAMY BUCKWHEAT PORRIDGE WITH CASHEW MILK

▲GF ▲WF ▲DF ▲VEG

MAKES 2½ CUPS (21½ FL OZ/625 ML)

This recipe can be eaten as an occasional breakfast dish over the first four-week period if you're craving a hot bowl of porridge, and then more regularly as your gut healing progresses.

> 1 cup (6¾ oz/195 g) creamy buckwheat, or regular buckwheat soaked overnight and rinsed
> 3 cups (26 fl oz/750 ml) filtered water
> pinch of Celtic sea salt
> 1 cup (9 fl oz/250 ml) cashew milk (see page 120)
> 1 handful of fresh berries, to serve (optional)

Put the buckwheat, water and salt in a medium saucepan over medium heat and bring to a boil. Reduce the heat to low and cook, covered, for 25 minutes or until tender, stirring regularly. Add a little more filtered water during cooking if necessary.

Add half the cashew milk and simmer for another 5 minutes or until the porridge has a thick, creamy consistency.

Spoon into a serving dish, pour over the remaining milk and top with fresh berries, if using.

RATATOUILLE BOWL

▲GF ▲WF ▲DF ▲SF ▲VEG

SERVES 1

There's something wondrous about a perfectly cooked eggplant, and you can't beat experiencing its tender silkiness in a bowl of steamy ratatouille. Eggplants also contain beneficial phenolic and flavonoid antioxidants that help protect against hypertension, type 2 diabetes, cardiovascular disease and liver toxicity.

1 tablespoon (20 ml) olive oil or butter, or 2 teaspoons ghee
1 scallion, finely chopped
2 cloves garlic, crushed
1 zucchini, diced
1 red pepper, seeded and diced
¼ eggplant, diced
4 tomatoes, chopped

Heat the oil, butter or ghee in a medium frying pan over medium heat. Add the scallion and garlic and cook, stirring frequently, for 2–3 minutes or until softened. Add the remaining ingredients and stir to combine. Reduce the heat to low and cook, covered, for 25 minutes or until the vegetables are tender.

Remove from the heat and allow to cool slightly, then purée in a food processor until smooth. If you prefer a chunkier version, and your tummy can take it, omit the processing step, as illustrated opposite.

MUSHY PEAS

▲ GF ▲ WF ▲ DF ▲ SF ▲ VEG

SERVES 4

These more-ish mushy peas will undo any memories of colorless, flavorless pea splutter. This is a beautiful comfort food that will satisfy a sweet tooth, fill you up and clean you out, thanks to its high fiber content.

- 2 tablespoons (40 ml) extra virgin olive oil or 1 tablespoon (20 ml) ghee
- 1 onion, chopped
- 2 cloves garlic, sliced
- 3⅓ cups (1 lb 2 oz/500 g) frozen peas
- 2 tablespoons (6 g) chopped mint
- 1 tablespoon (12 g) nutritional yeast flakes, to serve

Heat half the olive oil or ghee in a small frying pan over low–medium heat. Add the onion and garlic and cook for 4–5 minutes or until softened.

Heat the remaining olive oil in a medium saucepan over medium heat. Add the peas and cook, stirring occasionally, for 5 minutes. Add the onion mixture to the peas, reduce the heat to low and cook, covered, for 10 minutes or until the peas are soft. Mash or stir gently with a fork. Stir through the mint and serve topped with the yeast flakes.

SARDINE MASH

▲ GF ▲ WF ▲ DF ▲ SF

SERVES 1

Sardines might not immediately seem like the most joyous of foods, but they're so insanely beneficial you'll be sure to fall in love with them. They're rich in omega-3 fatty acids and energy-boosting vitamin B12, as well as minerals such as calcium, iron, magnesium, potassium and zinc. This mash is an inexpensive and nutrient-dense meal for when you feel like a boost.

3¼ oz (90 g) can sardines in extra virgin olive oil,
   drained and well mashed
½ medium avocado, pitted and peeled
1 teaspoon lemon juice
1 clove garlic, crushed
Celtic sea salt and freshly cracked black pepper, to taste
lemon halves, to serve

Put the sardines, avocado, lemon juice and garlic in a medium bowl, then mash with a fork until well combined or to your desired consistency. Season to taste and serve with lemon halves.

SCRAMBLED EGGS

▲GF ▲WF ▲DF ▲SF

SERVES 2

___

Eggs are one of nature's miraculously complete foods, and you can indulge in their sunny-colored creaminess while watching out for your digestive health. Switching regular cream or milk for calcium- and vitamin E–rich almond milk will provide a dairy-free version for weekend brunch. With wilted spinach and avocado on the side, this is a fun meal to have once or twice a week when you're healing in phase one – a chance to break away from soups for a day.

3 organic eggs
1 tablespoon (20 ml) almond milk (see page 123)
Celtic sea salt, to taste
1 tablespoon (20 ml) extra virgin olive oil
1 teaspoon grated lemon zest
pinch of nutmeg
freshly cracked black pepper, to taste
snipped chives, to serve (optional)

Whisk the eggs and almond milk in a bowl until well combined. Add sea salt to taste.

Heat the olive oil in a small frying pan over low-medium heat. Add the eggs and move them around the pan with a spatula so they don't stick to the bottom. When just set, add the lemon zest, nutmeg and some more salt, if desired. Serve immediately, garnished with pepper and chives, if using.

SQUASHY YELLOW SQUASH

▲ GF ▲ WF ▲ SF

SERVES 1

Squash made this way with gorgeous, beaming, yellow, garden-goddess-like buttons is hard to ignore. Take advantage of pattypan squash's seasonal abundance. Enjoy this as a side dish alongside bowls or soups.

1 cup (4½ oz/130 g) diced yellow button (pattypan) squash
1 tablespoon (14 g) butter
1 teaspoon lemon juice
pinch of Celtic sea salt
1–2 drops liquid stevia

Put the squash in a steamer over a saucepan of boiling water and steam for 5–6 minutes or until just tender. Allow to cool slightly, then transfer to a food processor with the butter, lemon juice and salt. Process until smooth, then add stevia to taste.

NOTE: *If not using right away, store in an airtight container in the fridge for up to 2 days.*

GREEN BEAN, TOMATO AND MINT MASH

▲GF ▲WF ▲DF ▲SF ▲VEG

SERVES 1

Super-simple to assemble, this faultless combo of highly flavor some vegetarian ingredients can be enjoyed as a sumptuous snack or satisfying side dish.

> 1 cup (4½ oz/125 g) steamed green beans
> 1 large tomato, chopped
> 1 small handful of mint leaves
> 1 tablespoon (20 ml) extra virgin olive oil
> Celtic sea salt and freshly cracked black pepper, to taste
> 2 tablespoons (40 ml) additive-free coconut milk (optional)
> small cherry tomatoes, to serve (optional)

Process the beans, tomato, mint and oil in a food processor until finely chopped. Season to taste and add the coconut milk if you prefer a creamier mix. Garnish with cherry tomatoes if using, and serve.

BROCCOLI MASH

▲GF ▲WF ▲SF

SERVES 3–4

Studies have linked broccoli in the diet with a decrease in gut levels of
E. coli and other bacterial strains associated with irritable bowel syndrome.
My yummy broccoli mash is an easy way to load up on these benefits and
celebrate this classic green.

> 2 heads broccoli, roughly chopped
> 2 tablespoons (28 g) butter
> 1 onion, chopped
> 3 cloves garlic, crushed
> Celtic sea salt and freshly cracked black pepper, to taste
> dulse flakes, to taste (optional)

Bring a large saucepan of water to the boil, then add the broccoli and cook
for 5–6 minutes or until al dente. Drain and set aside.

Melt the butter in a large saucepan over medium heat. Add the onion and
garlic and cook, stirring frequently, for 4–5 minutes or until soft.

Process the broccoli with the onion mixture in a food processor until smooth
or to your desired consistency. Season to taste and serve sprinkled with dulse
flakes, if using.

SUPERCHARGED TIP

....

*Boost the anti-inflammatory potency
of mashes by adding sardines or tuna
for extra omega-3s.*

....

MINTY SMASHED ZUCCHINI WITH GARLIC

▲GF ▲WF ▲DF ▲SF ▲VEG

SERVES 4

Bad-bacteria-busting garlic, immune-boosting onions, tummy-soothing mint and antioxidant-rich zucchini are combined in this powerful medley. It will not only supply your tummy with an array of healing properties, but is an ultra-comforting and flavorful vegie dish to tuck into.

4 large zucchini, cut into 3 inch (7.5 cm) lengths
¼ cup (2 fl oz/60 ml) extra virgin olive oil
1 onion, chopped
4 cloves garlic, crushed
2 tablespoons (12 g) roughly chopped mint
Celtic sea salt and freshly cracked black pepper, to taste

Put the zucchini in a steamer over a saucepan of boiling water and steam for 8–10 minutes or until soft. Drain and mash with a potato masher.

Heat the oil in a medium saucepan over medium heat. Add the onion and cook, stirring frequently, for 3–4 minutes or until translucent. Add the garlic and cook for 1 minute. Add the mashed zucchini and mint, and cook for another 5 minutes.

Season to taste and serve.

SAVORY SMASHED ROOT VEGETABLES

▲GF ▲WF ▲DF ▲SF ▲VEG

SERVES 4

This would have to be my favorite way to celebrate the diversity and deliciousness of the vegetables of winter. Grounding and satiating, this mash brings the warmth and comfort your body will crave in the cooler months. When you're in need of a sweet fix, this smash is better than reaching for a sugary treat.

1 medium orange sweet potato, peeled and cut into
    ¾–1¼ inch (2–3 cm) pieces
1 small turnip, peeled and cut into ½–¾ inch (1–2 cm) pieces
1 medium parsnip, peeled and cut into ½–¾ inch (1–2 cm) pieces
1 large carrot, peeled and cut into ½–¾ inch (1–2 cm) pieces
2 tablespoons (40 ml) extra virgin olive oil or butter
2 cloves garlic, sliced
⅓ cup (2½ fl oz/80 ml) additive-free coconut milk
2 tablespoons (24 g) nutritional yeast flakes
Celtic sea salt and freshly cracked black pepper, to taste

Put the sweet potato, turnip, parsnip and carrot in a large saucepan, then cover with filtered water and place over medium–high heat. Bring to a boil, then reduce the heat and simmer for 15–20 minutes or until the vegetables are soft. Drain.

Heat the olive oil or butter in a small saucepan over low heat. Add the garlic and coconut milk, then simmer for 5 minutes.

Put the cooked vegetables in a food processor with the coconut milk mixture and yeast flakes, then pulse until smooth. Season to taste and serve.

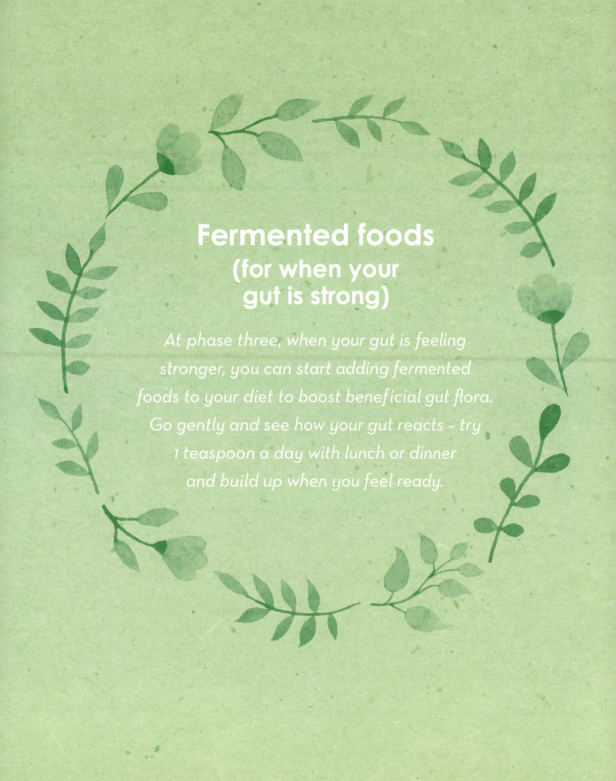

Fermented foods
(for when your gut is strong)

At phase three, when your gut is feeling stronger, you can start adding fermented foods to your diet to boost beneficial gut flora. Go gently and see how your gut reacts – try 1 teaspoon a day with lunch or dinner and build up when you feel ready.

CULTURED VEGETABLES

▲GF ▲WF ▲DF ▲SF ▲VEG

MAKES ABOUT 2 CUPS (17 FL OZ/500 ML)

Fermentation has been practiced by many societies since long before industrialization and processed foods. Adding a culture or salt to foods enables the growth of *Lactobacillus* bacterial cultures (probiotics), which preserve the food through the production of lactic acid. Fermented foods are full of healthy enzymes, minerals and live cultures that create a flourishing internal environment and help boost beneficial gut flora, all contributing to good digestion, a strong immune system and protection from toxic pollutants. They also help our bodies draw nutrients from our food.

Fermented veggies are great to eat alongside a meal to help your tummy digest your foods, especially as an accompaniment to starches and proteins.

You'll need one sterilized wide-mouthed, 4 cup (35 fl oz/1 L) capacity glass jar with lid (Mason jar).

> 1 small green cabbage, shredded
> 1 medium carrot, shredded (optional)
> 1 clove garlic, crushed
> 6 cups (52 fl oz/1.5 L) filtered water
> 1 tablespoon (18 g) finely ground Celtic sea salt
> pinch of freshly cracked black pepper
> 1 tablespoon (7 g) caraway seeds

Mix the cabbage, carrot, if using, and garlic in a large bowl. Transfer this mixture to the sterilized jar, leaving a 1 inch (2.5 cm) space at the top. Using a wooden spoon, push the mixture down to remove any air pockets.

Pour the water into a jug and add the salt, pepper and caraway seeds. Stir until the salt dissolves. Pour the liquid into the jar, leaving 1¼ inches (3 cm) at the top to allow room for expansion during fermentation. Push the vegetables down again with the wooden spoon, ensuring they're covered in the liquid. Put the lid on the jar, seal tightly and write the date on the jar.

Leave in a cool, dark, dry place for 3–5 days or until bubbles have started to form. Transfer to the fridge and enjoy for up to 4 weeks.

NOTE: *Start with a teaspoonful and only include with meals once you've reached phase three, the maintenance and restoration phase.*

KIMCHI

▲GF ▲WF ▲DF ▲SF ▲VEG

MAKES ABOUT 4 CUPS (35 FL OZ/1 L)

Fermented foods are nature's newest oldest superfoods, and their tangy flavors and spicy kick make them a perfect accompaniment to a meal once your gut is healed. Kimchi, a traditional Korean fermented food, offers a diverse range of wild bacterial strains that will benefit your inner ecology.

You'll need two sterilized wide-mouthed, 4 cup (35 fl oz/1 L) capacity glass jars with lids (Mason jars).

  1 small green cabbage, roughly chopped
  1 daikon, peeled and grated
  2 carrots, peeled and grated
  1 zucchini, grated
  ¼ cup (1 oz/30 g) chopped scallions
  1 inch (2.5 cm) piece ginger, peeled and grated
  2 cloves garlic, crushed
  1 heaping tablespoon (3 g) chili flakes
  ¼ cup (1¼oz/35 g) finely ground Celtic sea salt

Combine the cabbage, daikon, carrot and zucchini in a glass mixing bowl. Add the scallion, ginger, garlic, chili and salt, then massage the vegetables, using your hands, for about 4 minutes or until softened. Set aside for an hour or so to allow the salt to draw the moisture out of the vegetables.

Spoon the vegetables and liquid into the sterilized jars, pressing down to pack firmly and leaving 1 inch (2.5 cm) at the top to allow for expansion during fermentation. Put the lids on, seal tightly and write the date on the jars.

Store in a cool, dark, dry place for 3 days or until bubbles start to form. Transfer to the fridge and enjoy for up to 8 weeks.

SUPERCHARGED TIP

Always use a clean spoon each time you remove a little of any preserve from its jar.

EASY-TO-MAKE SAUERKRAUT

▲GF ▲WF ▲DF ▲SF ▲VEG

MAKES ABOUT 4 CUPS (35 FL OZ/1 L)

Homemade sauerkraut is full of the nutrients and phytochemicals that make cabbage a superstar ingredient, and the fermentation process makes them easier for the body to absorb. It also contains probiotics to recolonize your digestive tract, and is best enjoyed 1 tablespoon at a time, as a side with your meal.

You'll need two sterilized wide-mouthed, 4 cup (35 fl oz/1 L) capacity glass jars with lids (Mason jars).

- ½ green cabbage, finely sliced
- 8 cups (68 fl oz/2 L) filtered water
- 1 tablespoon (18 g) finely ground Celtic sea salt
- 2 cloves garlic, crushed
- 1 tablespoon (7 g) caraway seeds

Put the cabbage in the sterilized jars and press down with a wooden spoon to ensure it's tightly packed. Each jar should be three-quarters full.

Combine the water, salt, garlic and caraway seeds in a jug, stirring to dissolve the salt, then pour this mixture over the cabbage, leaving 1 inch (2.5 cm) at the top to allow for expansion during fermentation. Ensure the liquid is covering the cabbage, then put the lids on the jars and seal tightly. Write the date on the jars.

Store in a cool, dark, dry place for 3 days or until bubbles start to form. Transfer to the fridge and enjoy for up to 4 weeks.

SUPERCHARGED TIP

For fermented foods, always use filtered water, as chlorinated tap water can inhibit fermentation. Choose iodine-free salt with no anti-caking agents, which can also inhibit fermentation. Never omit the salt – it's a vital part of the preservation process.

FERMENTED SALSA

▲GF ▲WF ▲DF ▲SF ▲VEG

MAKES ABOUT 2 CUPS (17 FL OZ/500 ML)

This zingy and tangy salsa will pep you up and restore beneficial flora to your gut. Use as a dip with your favorite gluten-free cracker, add to steamed vegetables, serve alongside a salad, or plop on top of Scrambled Eggs (see page 218) or Fennel, Tomato and Roast Garlic Soup (see page 184).

You can buy vegetable starter at your local health food store or online. You'll need one sterilized wide-mouthed, 2 cups (17 fl oz/500 ml) capacity glass jar with a lid (Mason jar).

1 medium red (Spanish) onion, diced
3 tomatoes, diced
1 medium green pepper, seeded and diced
1 small red or green chili, finely chopped
2 cloves garlic, crushed
1 handful of fresh cilantro, finely chopped
¼ teaspoon ground cumin
1 tablespoon (20 ml) lime juice
grated zest of 1 lime
2 teaspoons Celtic sea salt (or ¼ cup/2 fl oz/60 ml vegetable starter culture and 1 teaspoon Celtic sea salt)

Thoroughly combine all the ingredients in a glass mixing bowl. Spoon into the sterilized jar, pressing down with a wooden spoon to pack firmly, leaving 1 inch (2.5 cm) at the top for expansion during fermentation. Put the lid on, seal tightly and write the date on the jar.

Store in a cool, dark, dry place for 3 days or until bubbles start to form. Transfer to the fridge and enjoy for up to 6 weeks.

HOMEMADE KOMBUCHA

▲GF ▲WF ▲DF ▲VEG

MAKES 4 CUPS (35 FL OZ/1 L)

Kombucha begins life as an ordinary sugary tea, but the addition of a SCOBY (symbiotic culture of bacteria and yeast) transforms it into a fermented drink. The SCOBY bacteria and yeast eat most of the sugar, yielding a drink full of natural probiotics that will dance around happily in your intestines. A small amount drunk daily has many gut-healing properties. Once you get the hang of making it, you can flavor it up with ginger and turmeric or even berries.

Purchase a SCOBY online or, if you're very lucky, a friend might give you one. You can buy kombucha online or at a health food store, although once you've made your first batch, you won't need to buy it any more. You'll also need a breathable cloth such as cheesecloth (I use a nut bag), a rubber band, and one sterilized wide-mouthed, 4 cup (35 fl oz/1 L) capacity glass jar with a lid (Mason jar).

> 4 cups (35 fl oz/1 L) filtered water
> 2 organic black tea bags
> ¼ cup (2 oz/55 g) organic sugar
> 1 SCOBY (see above)
> 3½ fl oz (100 ml) homemade or store-bought kombucha (see above)

Put the water in a medium saucepan over medium heat and bring to a boil. Remove from the heat, add the tea bags, and steep for 20 minutes. Remove the tea bags, add the sugar and stir until dissolved. Set aside to cool.

Pour the tea into the sterilized jar, then add the SCOBY and the kombucha. Cover with cheesecloth, secure with a rubber band and write the date on the jar.

Store undisturbed in a cool, dark, dry place for 7 days, then test it to see if it's ready. It should be fizzy and slightly sour/vinegary. If it's still sweet, let it ferment for a day or so longer (up to 10 days).

Once the kombucha is ready, carefully remove the SCOBY using a clean long-handled spoon and place it on a plate with a little of the liquid to stop it drying out (then use it to make another batch straight away). Pour out 3½ fl oz (100 ml) of the kombucha and keep aside to make another batch, then pour the remaining liquid into a jug through a sieve and then into a clean glass bottle with a lid. Secure the lid tightly and write the date on the bottle. The kombucha will keep in the fridge for 2–4 weeks.

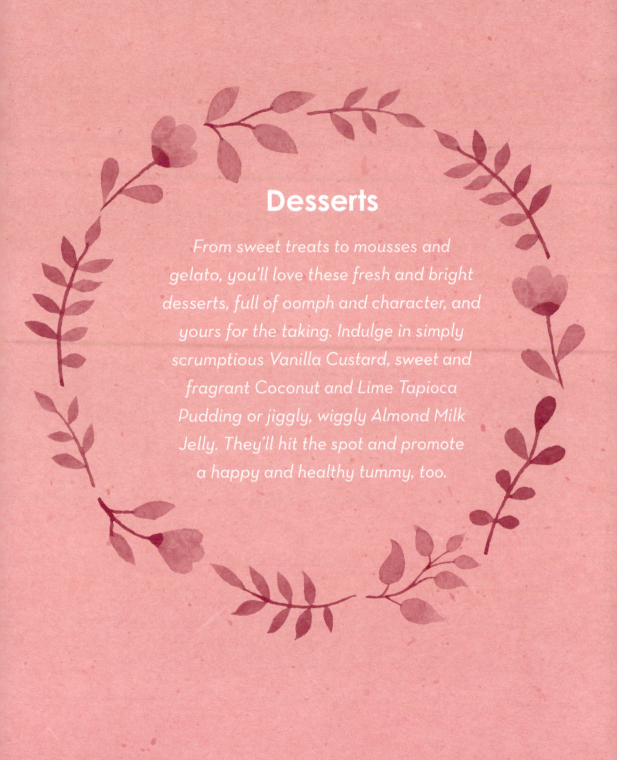

Desserts

From sweet treats to mousses and gelato, you'll love these fresh and bright desserts, full of oomph and character, and yours for the taking. Indulge in simply scrumptious Vanilla Custard, sweet and fragrant Coconut and Lime Tapioca Pudding or jiggly, wiggly Almond Milk Jelly. They'll hit the spot and promote a happy and healthy tummy, too.

BERRY SMOOTHIE BOWL

▲GF ▲WF ▲DF ▲VEG

SERVES 2

Berries are precious gems in the antioxidant department, and are delightfully sweet with a low fructose count, making them a gut-friendly dessert treat option. This fun recipe could easily double as a wholesome breakfast.

1 cup (5½ oz/155 g) frozen blueberries
½ cup (1 oz/25 g) baby spinach leaves
1 cup (5½ oz/150 g) frozen strawberries
1 cup (9 fl oz/250 ml) almond milk (see page 123)
1 tablespoon (14 g) almond butter
½ teaspoon alcohol-free vanilla extract

Purée all the ingredients in a blender until smooth and creamy. Spoon into serving dishes and serve immediately.

TAPIOCA PUDDING

▲GF ▲WF ▲DF ▲SF

SERVES 4

Tapioca is the starch that comes from the cassava plant, which is native to Brazil. It's a gentle, gluten-free alternative to starchy carbs and grains, which have the potential to increase the inflammation and mucosal damage that can lead to leaky gut.

  1/4 cup (1 3/4 oz/50 g) small pearl tapioca, soaked in filtered water
    for 30 minutes and then drained
  1 teaspoon stevia powder, or liquid stevia to taste
  1 organic egg, lightly beaten
  1/8 teaspoon ground nutmeg
  1/8 teaspoon ground cinnamon
  14 fl oz (400 ml) additive-free coconut milk
  1 cup (9 fl oz/250 ml) almond milk (see page 123)
  1 teaspoon alcohol-free vanilla extract

Place all the ingredients except the vanilla in a large bowl and whisk to combine. Set aside for 5 minutes to thicken.

Transfer the mixture to a small saucepan, then place over medium heat and bring to a boil. Continue to cook, stirring constantly, for 2–3 minutes or until the tapioca granules are translucent and soft.

Remove from the heat and stir through the vanilla. Serve when the dessert has your preferred combination of heat and thickness – the mixture will thicken as it cools.

ANTI-INFLAMMATORY SQUASH WHIP

▲GF ▲WF ▲DF ▲SF ▲VEG

SERVES 2

Squash has a neutral taste and smooth texture that makes it the perfect foundation for desserts. You won't even notice you're eating fiber-packed vegetables when you savor this sweet treat. It's intentionally packed with anti-inflammatory spices that will supercharge your healing.

1 cup Squashy Yellow Squash (see page 221)
1 inch (2.5 cm) piece of ginger, peeled and grated
⅛ teaspoon stevia powder
½ teaspoon ground cinnamon, plus extra to serve
½ teaspoon ground turmeric
¼ teaspoon alcohol-free vanilla extract
1 cup (9 fl oz/250 ml) additive-free coconut milk

Purée all the ingredients except the coconut milk in a blender until smooth and creamy, then add as much of the coconut milk as necessary for your preferred consistency. Serve with any remaining coconut milk, if desired, and a generous sprinkle of cinnamon.

VANILLA CUSTARD

▲GF ▲WF ▲SF

MAKES 1½ CUPS (13 FL OZ/375 ML)

There's nothing more soothing and indulgent than rich, velvety custard, but traditionally the white sugar and cream can leave your tummy tied up in knots. My version supplies the exact satisfaction custard should induce, but free of any awkward digestive complaints.

- ¾ cup (6 fl oz/185 ml) filtered water
- 1 teaspoon powdered gelatin
- 3 organic eggs
- 8 drops liquid stevia
- 4½ oz (125 g) unsalted organic butter, softened
- 1½ teaspoons alcohol-free vanilla extract

Pour the water into a small saucepan and sprinkle the gelatin over the top. Set aside for a minute or until the gelatin softens. Put the saucepan over medium heat and stir constantly with a wooden spoon for 2–3 minutes or until the gelatin has dissolved.

Pour the gelatin mixture into a blender, then add the eggs, stevia, butter and vanilla. Blend on low speed for 2 minutes or until pale and thick.

Spoon the custard into an airtight container and chill in the fridge. Stir before using. The custard will keep in the fridge for 3 days.

NOTE: *To make Chai Custard, add ¼ teaspoon ground cinnamon, ¼ teaspoon ground nutmeg and ⅓ teaspoon ground cardamom.*

LEMON AND BLUEBERRY ICE CREAM

▲GF ▲WF ▲DF ▲VEG

SERVES 2–3

Load up on alkalizing, detoxifying lemon and antioxidant-rich blueberries in this sugar-free ice cream. Velvety, vitamin E–rich avocado and gut-flora-friendly coconut carry the zingy flavors perfectly. The frozen berries create an ice-cream texture without any freezing step. It's a refreshing way to finish off your dinner.

1 cup (5½ oz/155 g) frozen blueberries
¼ cup (2 fl oz/60 ml) additive-free coconut milk
½ teaspoon alcohol-free vanilla extract
juice of ½ lemon
½ medium avocado, pitted and peeled

Purée all the ingredients in a blender until smooth and creamy. Serve immediately.

COCONUT AND LIME TAPIOCA PUDDING

▲GF ▲WF ▲DF ▲SF

SERVES 2

Whisk yourself away to the tropics with this sweet sensation that will leave you dreaming of island sunsets. Coconut is at the top of my list for gut-friendly foods, as it boasts amazing antimicrobial, antifungal and antiviral properties, thanks to its precious healthy saturated fats: lauric, capric and caprylic acids.

½ cup (3¼ oz/95 g) small pearl tapioca
2½ cups (21½ fl oz/625 ml) almond milk (see page 123)
¼ teaspoon alcohol-free vanilla extract
pinch of Celtic sea salt
9½ fl oz (270 ml) can additive-free coconut milk
2 large organic egg yolks, lightly beaten
⅛ teaspoon stevia powder
1 tablespoon (6 g) grated lime zest, plus extra to serve
2 tablespoons (40 ml) lime juice

Heat the tapioca, almond milk, vanilla extract and salt in a medium saucepan over medium heat. Bring to a simmer and cook, stirring occasionally, for 10–15 minutes or until the tapioca is translucent. Stir in the coconut milk, then remove from the heat.

In a large bowl, combine the egg yolks with the stevia, then add to the tapioca mixture gradually, stirring constantly. Stir in the lime zest and juice. Put the saucepan over medium heat and cook, stirring constantly, until the mixture has thickened.

Refrigerate until set, then serve garnished with extra lime zest.

ALMOND MILK JELLY CUP

▲GF ▲WF ▲DF ▲SF

MAKES 1 CUP (9 FL OZ/250 ML)

Gelatin is a good source of protein and contains eighteen protein-building amino acids. It's a great ingredient to include in your gut-healing arsenal, as it seals the digestive tract to help boost nutrient absorption.

> 1 cup (9 fl oz/250 ml) almond milk (see page 123)
> 2 teaspoons powdered gelatin
> ¼ teaspoon vanilla powder
> ½ teaspoon powdered stevia

Put half the almond milk and the gelatin in a small saucepan over low heat. Whisk briskly until the gelatin is dissolved. Remove from the heat and add the remaining almond milk along with the vanilla and stevia, and whisk to combine.

Pour into one or two glasses or jelly molds and refrigerate until set. The jelly can be stored in an airtight container in the fridge for 1–2 weeks.

KEFIR YOGURT

▲GF ▲WF ▲DF ▲SF ▲VEG

SERVES 2

Boost your inner ecosystem with the beneficial bacteria in this delicious yogurt to keep your immune system strong.

You'll need a sterilized glass bowl or large jar, a blender, a strainer, a square of cheesecloth, an elastic band and a wooden spoon. (Avoid using metal, and store in a glass jar.)

> 3 young coconuts, at room temperature
> 2 dairy-free probiotic capsules or 1 tablespoon
>   dairy-free probiotic powder
> liquid stevia or stevia powder, to taste
> fresh berries, to serve (optional)

Open the coconuts and strain the coconut water into a bowl. Set aside.

Scrape out the coconut flesh, trying not to include any husk, and place in a blender. Add the coconut water and blend until creamy – it should have the consistency of yogurt.

Pour the mixture into a glass bowl and add the contents of the probiotic capsules or the probiotic powder.

Cover the bowl with cheesecloth, securing it with the elastic band, and put in a cool, dry, dark place for 1–2 days. When ready, it should taste fairly sharp without a hint of sweetness.

Add stevia to taste, then refrigerate and enjoy over the next 7 days. Serve with fresh berries, if using.

CHOCOLATY MOUSSE

▲GF ▲WF ▲DF ▲SF ▲VEG

SERVES 2

This decadent, rich, chocolate mousse will give any regular cream-filled variety a run for its money. Cacao is also a highly beneficial and gut-friendly food; studies have shown that gut bacteria transform components of cacao into anti-inflammatory chemicals that benefit your health.

1 ripe avocado, pitted and peeled
¼ cup (2 fl oz/60 ml) almond milk (see page 123)
1 tablespoon (7 g) chia seeds
1 teaspoon alcohol-free vanilla extract
⅓ cup (1 oz/30 g) cacao powder
8 drops liquid stevia
fresh berries, to serve (optional)

Combine all the ingredients except the berries in a blender and blend for 30 seconds, until smooth and creamy. Spoon into bowls and chill slightly before serving topped with fresh berries, if desired.

NOTE: *If you suffer from adrenal fatigue, consume cacao in moderation, preferably in the morning.*

ALOE VERA JELLY

▲ GF ▲ WF ▲ DF ▲ SF ▲ VEG

SERVES 1

This refreshing jelly is very soothing for the gut but, as it's a mild laxative, don't overindulge if you have a tendency for diarrhea. Play with the flavors by replacing the vanilla with chopped mint, a favorite spice or even berries.

12 fl oz (350 ml) aloe vera juice
1–2 teaspoons agar-agar
¼ teaspoon alcohol-free vanilla extract
liquid stevia, to taste
shredded coconut, to taste (optional)

Warm the aloe vera juice in a medium saucepan over medium heat, then add the agar-agar and stir until it dissolves. Continue stirring for a couple of minutes. When the mixture starts to boil, remove from the heat, add the vanilla extract and stevia, then pour into ice-cube trays.

Top with the coconut, if using, then refrigerate until set.

SMASHED RASPBERRY

▲ GF   ▲ WF   ▲ DF   ▲ VEG

MAKES 1½ CUPS (13 FL OZ/375 ML)

Raspberries are a beautifully tart and refreshingly sweet treat low in yeast-feeding sugars, making them an excellent replacement for confectionery, conventional sweets and even high-fructose fruits such as bananas. Be on the lookout for the freshest (or fresh frozen) organic raspberries, as studies have shown them to contain higher levels of antioxidants.

1 cup (5½ oz/155 g) natural cashews,
   pre-soaked (see page 120) and drained
½ cup (2¼ oz/60 g) frozen raspberries, plus extra, mashed (optional)
½ teaspoon alcohol-free vanilla extract
¼ teaspoon ground cinnamon
pinch of Celtic sea salt

Purée all the ingredients in a food processor until smooth and creamy. Stir through extra raspberries, if using. Serve immediately.

L–R: Raspberry and Lime Pudding, Raspberry Gelato

RASPBERRY AND LIME PUDDING

▲ GF ▲ WF ▲ DF ▲ VEG

SERVES 2

For me, the word "pudding" conjures up images of something incredibly joyous, sweet and a little bit on the naughty side. This fruity pudding is all of the above, but its naughtiness is only in its lip-smacking sweetness. You can indulge in this dessert knowing that every ounce of it is bringing life to your intestinal cells.

2 cups (9 oz/250 g) frozen raspberries
grated zest and juice of 1 lime
½ teaspoon alcohol-free vanilla extract
¾ cup (4¼ oz/120 g) natural cashews,
   pre-soaked (see page 120) and drained
½ cup (4 fl oz/125 ml) additive-free coconut milk, chilled
⅛ teaspoon stevia powder
small pinch of Celtic sea salt

Purée all the ingredients in a food processor. Serve immediately.

RASPBERRY GELATO

▲ GF ▲ WF ▲ DF ▲ VEG

SERVES 3

Skip the local gelateria. With this gorgeously pink and silky-smooth substitute, you can savor every last mouthful with zero guilt and zero tummy upsets.

1¼ cups (6¾ oz/195 g) natural cashews,
   pre-soaked (see page 120) and drained
2 teaspoons alcohol-free vanilla extract
¾ cup (3¼ oz/90 g) frozen raspberries
1 tablespoon lemon juice
6 drops liquid stevia
½ cup (4 fl oz/125 ml) additive-free coconut milk

Purée all the ingredients in a food processor until smooth. Transfer to three individual ice-cream molds or ramekins and place in the freezer for 2 hours or until frozen. Run a warm knife around the outside edge of the molds, then turn each one out into a bowl, or scoop into a dish, and serve immediately.

AVOCADO ICE CREAM

▲GF ▲WF ▲DF ▲SF ▲VEG

SERVES 2

This is a recipe you could do blindfolded with one arm tied behind your back. It's that easy, but so utterly delicious and creamy. Avocados are also ridiculously beneficial; full of monounsaturated fats and vitamin E, they're easy on the gut lining, too. You can now happily wave your regular dairy-filled chemical cocktail goodbye and swap it with this soothing dessert.

1 avocado, pitted and peeled
½ cup (4 fl oz/125 ml) additive-free coconut milk, chilled
1 tablespoon (20 ml) lemon juice
¼ teaspoon alcohol-free vanilla extract
6 drops liquid stevia

Purée all the ingredients in a blender until smooth and creamy.

Churn the mixture in an ice-cream machine according to the manufacturer's instructions, or cover and freeze for 1–2 hours or until just frozen, then stir vigorously or beat with a hand mixer. Return the ice cream to the freezer, then stir or beat every 30 minutes two or three more times. Return to the freezer until completely frozen.

BAKED BLUEBERRY CUSTARDS

▲ GF   ▲ WF   ▲ DF

SERVES 4

Ultra-comforting and soft like a big downy blanket, this is one of my favorite sweet comfort foods to cuddle up to at the end of a cold day. Coconut milk is an excellent replacement for traditional dairy, making an allergy- and digestive-system-friendly custard.

14 fl oz (400 ml) can additive-free coconut milk
4 organic egg yolks
1 teaspoon alcohol-free vanilla extract
8 drops liquid stevia
1 cup (5½ oz/155 g) blueberries

Preheat the oven to 275°F/gas mark 1 (140°C).

Heat the coconut milk in a medium saucepan over medium heat for 2–3 minutes or until just warmed.

Meanwhile, whisk the egg yolks to ribbon stage (when you lift the whisk the mixture falls slowly and forms a ribbon that holds its shape for a while). Slowly add the coconut milk to the egg, then return to the saucepan and place over medium heat, stirring constantly, until it starts to thicken. Remove from the heat, then stir through the vanilla extract and stevia.

Divide the blueberries between four ramekins or ovenproof bowls, then pour the egg mixture over the top. Place the serving dishes in a baking dish, then pour enough boiling water into the baking dish to come halfway up the sides of the ramekins.

Bake for 30–35 minutes or until the custards wobble when shaken gently. Allow to cool, then refrigerate until you're ready to serve.

APPENDIX

THE HEAL YOUR GUT PROGRAM

I hope you've enjoyed the information and recipes provided in this book. If you'd like to continue to heal your gut, there are brand new recipes appearing every week on my blog. The Heal Your Gut Program can be undertaken again whenever you feel that your gut needs maintenance or when you're looking to bring your gut flora back to a healthy balance. Come and join the Heal Your Gut Program online at superchargedfood.com and connect with the Supercharged Food community.

COACH WITH ME

If you need a bit of extra help with your wellness goals, I offer personal health coaching sessions in person or via Skype. The sessions involve guiding you to make food and lifestyle choices to bring your life back into balance. I offer a step-by-step holistically based personal health program to enable you to heal your body at a cellular level and to reach your current and future health goals. If you'd like a personal session, contact me via email on lee@superchargedfood.com

SOCIALIZE WITH ME

blog: superchargedfood.com/blog

share: superchargedfood.com

 like: facebook.com/superchargedfood

 follow: twitter.com/LeeSupercharged

 insta: instagram.com/leesupercharged

 link: linkedin.com/in/leesupercharged

 watch: youtube.com/leeholmes67

NOTES

For references to my website, see **superchargedfood.com**.
For references to my blog, see **superchargedfood.com/blog**.

PART ONE: THE VITAL IMPORTANCE OF YOUR GUT

INSIDE YOUR GUT

p. 6   In fact, many researchers are beginning to say ...: A. Fasano & T. Shea-Donohue, 'Mechanisms of Disease: the role of intestinal barrier function in the pathogenesis of gastrointestinal autoimmune diseases', *Nature Clinical Practice Gastroenterology and Hepatology*, vol. 2, no. 9, September 2005, pp. 416–22, direct-ms.org/sites/default/files/Fasano intestinal barrier autoimmunity.pdf

p. 7   Research has found that the presence ...: V.K. Ridaura et al., 'Gut microbiota from twins discordant for obesity modulate metabolism in mice', *Science*, vol. 341, no. 6150, 2013, ncbi.nlm.nih.gov/pubmed/24009397; Current research by senior scientists ...: 'Human food project: anthropology of microbes', 2012, humanfoodproject.com/americangut.

CANDIDA AND THE GUT

p. 10   It's been shown to be effective against 24 out of 26 strains ...: D.K. Sandhu et al., 'Sensitivity of yeasts isolated from cases of vaginitis to aqueous extracts of garlic', *Mycoses*, vol. 23, no. 12, December 1980, pp. 691–98, onlinelibrary.wiley.com/doi/10.1111/j.1439-0507.1980.tb01776.x/abstract; Research from the University of Illinois ...: S. Hooda et al., '454 pyrosequencing reveals a shift in fecal microbiota of healthy adult men consuming polydextrose or soluble corn fiber', *Journal of Nutrition*, vol. 142, no. 7, July 2012, pp. 1259–65, ncbi.nlm.nih.gov/pubmed/22649263.

HEALING AND MAINTAINING A HEALTHY GUT BARRIER

p. 12   Although conventional medicine in the past ...: J. Visser et al., 'Tight junctions, intestinal permeability, and autoimmunity: celiac disease and type 1 diabetes paradigms', *Annals of the New York Academy of Sciences*, vol. 1165, May 2009, pp. 195–205, ncbi.nlm.nih.gov/pubmed/19538307.

p. 15   Scientific evidence now shows that the types of food ...: K.M. Maslowski & C.R. Mackay, 'Diet, gut microbiota and immune responses', *Nature Immunology*, vol. 12, no. 1, January 2011, pp. 5–9, 211.144.68.84:9998/91keshi/Public/File/26/12-1/pdf/ni0111-5.pdf.

p. 16   Research has gone so far as to show ...: P. Bercik et al., 'The anxiolytic effect of *Bifidobacterium longum* NCC3001 involves vagal pathways for gut–brain communication', *Neurogastroenterology and Motility*, vol. 23, no. 12, December 2011, pp. 1132–39, ncbi.nlm.nih.gov/pubmed/21988661; Other fascinating scientific findings ...: M. Maes, 'The cytokine hypothesis of depression: inflammation, oxidative and nitrosative stress (IO&NS) and leaky gut as new targets for adjunctive treatments in depression', *Neuroendocrinology Letters*, vol. 29, no. 3, June 2008, pp. 287–91, ncbi.nlm.nih.gov/pubmed/18580840.

p. 17   Research continues to link the state of the gut ...: R.E. Ley et al., 'Microbial ecology: human gut microbes associated with obesity', *Nature*, vol. 444, December 2006, pp. 1022–23, nature.com/nature/journal/v444/n7122/abs/4441022a.html.

FACTORS THAT DAMAGE THE GUT

p. 18   Science now shows that a number of ...: S Drago et al., 'Gliadin, zonulin and gut permeability: effects on celiac and non-celiac intestinal mucosa and intestinal cell lines', *Scandinavian Journal of Gastroenterology*, vol. 41, no. 4, April 2006, pp. 408–19, ncbi.nlm.nih.gov/pubmed/16635908; The wheat we consume today ...: W. Davis, *Wheat Belly: Lose the Wheat, Lose the Weight, and Find Your Path Back to Health*, Rodale, New York, 2011.

p. 20   The over-prescription and overuse of antibiotics ...: M. Blaser, 'Antibiotic overuse: stop the killing of beneficial bacteria', *Nature*, vol. 476, no. 7361, August 2011,

pp. 393–94, nature.com/nature/journal/
v476/n7361/full/476393a.html; Antibiotics
are known to cause diarrhea …: Mayo Clinic,
'Antibiotic-associated diarrhea', June 2013,
mayoclinic.org/diseases-conditions/antibiotic-
associated-diarrhea/basics/causes/con-
20023556.

p. 21   This kind of short-term stress can be dealt
with …: M.T. Bailey et al., 'Exposure to a social
stressor alters the structure of the intestinal
microbiota: implications for stressor-induced
immunomodulation', *Brain, Behavior, and
Immunology*, vol. 25, no. 3, March 2011, pp.
397–407, ncbi.nlm.nih.gov/pubmed/21040780.

PART TWO: HEALING AND TREATMENT PROTOCOL

PHASE TWO: DETOX YOUR BODY

p. 76   It's also antibacterial, antiviral, antifungal and
anti-parasitic (oil of oregano): M. Force et al.,
'Inhibition of enteric parasites by emulsified
oil of oregano in vivo', *Phytotherapy
Research*, vol. 14, no. 3, May 2000, pp. 213–14,
ncbi.nlm.nih.gov/pubmed/10815019.

p. 80   Echinacea increases the level of a
chemical called properdin …: L.S. Kim
et al., 'Immunological activity of larch
arabinogalactan and Echinacea: a preliminary,
randomized, double-blind, placebo-
controlled trial', *Alternative Medicine Review*,
vol. 7, no. 2, April 2002, pp. 138–49, ncbi.nlm.
nih.gov/pubmed/11991793; Cinnamon: an
antimicrobial that was found …: H.K. Kwon
et al., 'Cinnamon extract suppresses
experimental colitis through modulation
of antigen-presenting cells', *World
Journal of Gastroenterology*, vol. 17, no. 8,
February 2011, pp. 976-86, ncbi.nlm.nih.gov/
pubmed/21451725.

PHASE THREE: MAINTAIN AND RESTORE WITH FOOD

p. 88   Apart from helping out the brain as well
as the immune system …: Y. Perrin et
al., 'Comparison of two oral probiotic
preparations in a randomized crossover trial
highlights a potentially beneficial effect of
Lactobacillus paracasei NCC2461 in patients
with allergic rhinitis', *Clinical and Translational
Allergy*, vol. 4, no. 1, January 2014, article 1,
ncbi.nlm.nih.gov/pubmed/24393277.

PHASE FOUR: DETOX YOUR LIFE

p. 90   Evidence also suggests that our gut bacteria
…: P.C. Konturek et al., 'Stress and the gut:
pathophysiology, clinical consequences,
diagnostic approach and treatment options',
Journal of Physiology and Pharmacology,
vol. 62, no. 6, 2011, pp. 591–99, jpp.krakow.
pl/journal/archive/12_11/pdf/591_12_11_article.
pdf; Sunlight and exposing your bare feet …:
M.N. Mead, 'Benefits of sunlight: a bright
spot for human health', *Environmental Health
Perspectives*, vol. 116, no. 4, April 2008,
pp. A160–67, ncbi.nlm.nih.gov/pmc/
articles/PMC2290997; It also boosts social
connectedness …: R. Grimm et al., *The
Health Benefits of Volunteering: A Review of
Recent Research*, Corporation for National
and Community Service, New York, 2007,
nationalservice.gov/pdf/07_0506_hbr.pdf;

p 91   Chemicals in household cleaning products
…: A. Gorman, *Household Hazards: A Look
at the Potential Hazards of Chemicals in
Household Cleaning Products and Their
Association with Asthma and Reproductive
Harm*, Women's Voices for the Earth,
2007, womensvoices.org/wp-content/
uploads/2010/06/HazardsReport.pdf.

INDEX

ACKNOWLEDGMENTS

I wrote this book for you, not anyone else. I hope that when you read it, whenever you're ready, whether you're at a turning point in your life or you've perhaps just plucked it from your local library's bookshelf out of general interest, that you'll benefit and be encouraged by the words on the pages and the healing recipes. Life is a delight and an adventure, and to live it to its full potential sometimes you need to become a tightrope walker and find the path that resonates with you. When you listen to your body and walk to the beat of your own drum, miraculous things can happen.

Heartfelt thanks to all of the hardworking and dedicated people who helped to bring this book into your hands.

My wonderful publishers Murdoch Books and the ethereal Diana Hill, who is a delight to work with. The world's best publicist, Christine Farmer, who is a constant source of support and encouragement. The stylishly creative and top-notch team of Hugh Ford, Miriam Steenhauer, Virginia Birch, Nicola Young, Matt Hoy, Robert Gorman, Sue Hines and Patrizia Di Biase-Dyson.

Thanks so much to the photographic and production team who captured my vision so eloquently and brought this book to life: foodie extraordinaire Grace Campbell, photographer Cath Muscat and super-stylist Sarah O'Brien.

Special thanks to Louise Cornege, Juliet Potter, Howard Porter, Georgie Bridge, Rosana Lauria, Kristy Plumridge, Hilary Davis, Cindy Luken, Jessica Lowe, Lucie Robazza, Pia Larsen, Grahame Grassby, Mike Conway and Cindy Sciberras.

Big thanks and love to my family: Alex von Kotze, Roxy, Arizona, Carol, Lorraine, Clive and Ben. To my world and my greatest achievement, Tamsin Holmes, so proud of the young woman you are becoming and congratulations on getting into Sydney University to study philosophy. My best friend and my dreamboat partner, Justin, you are my inspiration, and thank you for your never-ending supply of love and support.

Yours affectionately,
Lee xo

Quarto is the authority on a wide range of topics.

Quarto educates, entertains and enriches the lives of our readers—enthusiasts and lovers of hands-on living.

www.QuartoKnows.com

First published in the United States of America in 2016 by
Fair Winds Press, an imprint of
Quarto Publishing Group USA Inc.
100 Cummings Center
Suite 406-L
Beverly, Massachusetts 01915-6101
Telephone: (978) 282-9590
Fax: (978) 283-2742
QuartoKnows.com
Visit our blogs at QuartoKnows.com

20 19 18 17 16   1 2 3 4 5

ISBN: 978-1-59233-754-5

Library of Congress Cataloging-in-Publication Data available

Printed in China

IMPORTANT
Those who might be at risk from the effects of salmonella poisoning (the elderly, pregnant women, young children and those suffering from immune deficiency diseases) should consult their doctor with any concerns about eating raw eggs.

OVEN GUIDE
You may find cooking times vary depending on the oven you are using. For fan-forced ovens, as a general rule, set the oven temperature to 35°F (20°C) lower than indicated in the recipe.

MEASURES GUIDE
We have used 20 ml (4 teaspoon) tablespoon measures. If you are using a 15 ml (3 teaspoon) tablespoon add an extra teaspoon of the ingredient for each tablespoon specified.

DISCLAIMER
This book is designed to provide the reader with information as a general guide to healing the gut. It is sold under the understanding that the publisher and author are not engaged in rendering professional medical services. The protocol in this book has been adopted and implemented during the author's own healing. If you have concerns about your health and medical expert assistance is required, it is advisable that you contact your medical practitioner or healthcare provider. The author and publisher are not liable or responsible to any person or entity with respect to loss or damage caused directly or indirectly by the information contained in this book.